GUIDE TO VEGETARIAN RESTAURANTS IN ISRAEL

GUIDE TO VEGETARIAN RESTAURANTS IN ISRAEL

BY MARK WEINTRAUB

VRg.

The Vegetarian Resource Group
Baltimore, Maryland
1996

Acknowledgements:

I would like to thank Charles Stahler of The Vegetarian Resource Group, Lauren Fisher for all her help in the early stages of this project, members of the Jewish Vegetarian Society, local offices of the Ministry of Tourism, Tami Moskowitz and of course, my wife Ina who is my vegetarian partner in life and whose insight was, as always, helpful and inspiring. I would also like to thank Carole Hamlin, Mary Jamieson, Israel Mossman, Richard Schwartz, Rosanne Silverman, and Debra Wasserman for proofreading the manuscript and Janet Steinberg for the cover art.

Project Supervisor: Charles Stahler

Front Cover: Janet Steinberg

Back Cover, Typeset, Illustrations, & Design:
    Vonnie Winslow Crist, Win-Cri Enterprises

Copyright 1996 Mark Weintraub

Published by The Vegetarian Resource Group,
    P. O. Box 1463, Baltimore, Maryland 21203

Library of Congress Cataloging-in-Publication Data:
Guide To Vegetarian Restaurants In Israel/Mark Weintraub

Library of Congress Catalog Card Number: 95-060839

ISBN 0-931411-16-5

Printed in the United States of America
10 9 8 7 6 5 4 3 2 1

 • We would like to hear from you!! Write and let us know if you found an interesting spot that we did not include, a restaurant out of business, or your comments about the food/service/atmosphere at the restaurants you visited. Please send comments to: The Vegetarian Resource Group, PO Box 1463, Baltimore, MD 21203 United States of America. E-Mail address is: TheVRG@aol.com

CONTENTS

Introduction   7

Restaurant Listings

    Jerusalem   11

    Tel Aviv   23

    Jaffa   40

    Haifa   42

    Tiberias   47

    The Galilee: Resorts & Restaurants   50

      Moshav Amirim   52

    Eilat   55

Health Food Stores in Israel

    Jerusalem   58

    Tel Aviv   59

    Greater Tel Aviv   60

    Haifa   61

Useful Contacts in Israel

    Animal Welfare   62

    Vegetarian/Vegan Societies   64

    Environmental Organizations   64

A Vegetarian Hebrew-English Dictionary

    Food Related Terms   65

    General Terms   66

Foods and Definitions of Foods
    Commonly Found in Israel   67

The International Jewish Vegetarian Society   70

About the Author   72

Resources in the United States   73

What is The Vegetarian Resource Group?   74

Other Books Available from
    The Vegetarian Resource Group   75

Subscribe to The Vegetarian Journal   81

Israeli Vegetarian
    Restaurant Guide Survey Form   84

Travel Notes   86

To Order Additional Copies of
    Guide to Vegetarian Restaurants in Israel   88

INTRODUCTION

Living in Israel for the past six years, I have encountered many different cultural experiences and surprises. The writing of this guide presented a few that were totally unexpected.

The method originally selected to acquire the data for this guide was the compilation of a survey to be filled out by the restaurants chosen and returned along with a copy of their menu. To my surprise, only a few restaurants responded! I was a bit dumbfounded, since there was no charge for inclusion in this guide (typically restaurants pay to be included) and the questionnaire was quite simple, translated into both English and Hebrew.

So, I decided to visit practically all the establishments which are listed in this book. When I inquired into why the restaurants did not respond, I found two reasons. The first was an Israeli attitude towards non-proliferation of information, or more plainly put - no communicating in writing or "getting back to you." A second reason was that *many owners did not really understand what vegetarianism is and did not think that they belonged in such a book.* Many who considered (or advertised) themselves as vegetarian restaurants did serve some type of animal product -- usually fish. Almost none of the restaurants I visited (except for the strict vegetarian ones) knew what veganism was or that organic products are more than fresh vegetables. (In one instance, I made a connection between a restaurant and an organic vegetable producer.) This provided a wonderful outreach opportunity to educate those in the food business about these concepts, and I can safely say that this guide benefits those on both sides of the restaurant table.

There are a few general rules that I wish to share with the vegetarian traveler to Israel:

TYPES OF RESTAURANTS:
Options for the *vegetarian** or *vegan*** purists are limited to a few establishments in each area. Although the first dietary law prescribed in the Bible is a purely vegetarian one, we have evolved to a point where the separation of milk and meat creates two types of restaurants; *dairy restaurants* (which serve non-meat products and fish) and *meat restaurants* (which serve beef and fowl but no milk products). This separation makes our job to find vegetarian options easier. For example, in Jerusalem, one can feel safe to find a suitable option in a dairy restaurant or ethnic restaurant which offers vegetarian options. However, in the other cities listed in this book, even that distinction is not so clear. My objective has been to go "behind the scenes," analyzing menus and interviewing restaurant personnel to determine options for both vegetarians and vegans, with an emphasis on different types of dining atmospheres. As much as possible, I tried to include restaurants that are frequented by tourists and local Israelis -- we all enjoy eating!!

KOSHER CERTIFICATION:
Kosher certification of restaurants is controlled by the Rabbinate, a quasi-governmental institution. In the simplest terms, a restaurant receives certification if it does not serve milk and meat on the same premises, uses kosher products, and is not open on the Sabbath. Restaurants with kosher certification are designated in this guide with further indication if the restaurant is *Glatt****. In Jerusalem, most restaurants are kosher, since many residents are religious. Tel Aviv and the other major cities are quite another story, as people venture out on Friday night and Saturday and restaurants are open. Some restaurant owners who do not have kosher certification claim that they use kosher products, but do not have certification because they are open on the Sabbath. This is up to your discretion, and it is advisable to ask the owner to show you his kosher certificate or inquire if the products used are kosher. You might also want to observe whether others who are concerned about kashrut eat there.

HOURS:
The Israeli work week is from Sunday until Thursday night (or Friday noon). The Sabbath (*Shabbat* in Hebrew) is observed from sundown Friday night until sundown Saturday night. As the time for sundown differs by the season, closing and

opening times on "Shabbat" are indicated as one hour before or after Shabbat's entrance or exit. You can find the exact times of Shabbat on the front page of Friday's English newspaper.

RESERVATIONS: The most popular nights for Israelis to go out are Thursdays, Fridays, and Saturdays. Therefore, it is highly recommended to make reservations if you wish to go out to a popular night spot at these times. I have indicated which restaurants have suggested that reservations are desirable during the week.

PRICES/METHOD OF PAYMENT: Here I have tried to estimate the average cost of an entrée both in Israeli Shekels (NIS) and US Dollars in parentheses. (The exchange rate used is $1 U.S. = 3 NIS). This price will certainly change, but at least it is a general comparative figure. Methods of acceptable payment include Credit Cards, Foreign Currency (which usually means dollars), and the least favored method of payment -- Traveler's Checks. If you intend to pay with traveler's checks, it is advisable to bring your passport.

TELEPHONE CALLS: Israeli area codes are two digit with the preface of "0". They are listed in parenthesis next to the local phone number. If you are in the town where the restaurant is located, there is no need to dial the area code. If you wish to dial from overseas, begin dialing with the Israeli country code ("972"), drop the zero in front of the city code and continue with the local phone number. For example, if you wish to dial the Jewish Vegetarian Society's Jerusalem Headquarters which is (02) 611-114 in Israel, you should dial 972-2-611-114. (From New York and other U. S. locations, you must dial 011 before the 972.) Be sure to check with your long distance operator as to the time difference between your home and Israel.

OTHER ITEMS OF INTEREST: This guide notes if the restaurant uses organic products, has limitations on smoking, and which meals are served. Also included are lists of resorts, health food stores, local vegetarian and animal rights organizations, and a Hebrew - English vegetarian survival dictionary.

A final word about the rules and definitions listed above. When I first made *aliyah* (immigrated) to Israel, I was given the following piece of advice: "In the Middle East, *Yes* doesn't really mean *Yes* and *No* doesn't really mean *No*." The meaning is that no matter what is written, everything is negotiable. Therefore, it is quite advisable (and acceptable by local Israelis) to inquire into how each dish is made, and ask that the dish be prepared according to your standards as a vegetarian or a vegan. Many restaurants indicated a willingness to do so. Remember, the more vocal we are, the more the restaurants will be flexible to our demands as customers and offer more vegetarian and vegan dishes.

What else can I say, but these two expressions in Hebrew: *B'teavon* (Bon Appetit!) and *Nisia Tovah!* (Have a good trip!!).

Mark Weintraub

Vegetarian is defined as a diet without meat, fish, and fowl.

** *Vegan* is a vegetarian diet that excludes all animal products such as dairy and eggs.

***Glatt* literally means smooth, indicating that meat comes from an animal whose lung has been found to be free of all adhesions. Currently, *Glatt Kosher* has come to be used more broadly as a consumer phrase meaning kosher without question (from The Orthodox Union).

JERUSALEM

This section needs little introduction since Jerusalem has much to offer vegetarians. As almost all restaurants in Jerusalem are Kosher, you can certainly find a convenient meal at any dairy restaurant in the city. There also is a small but nice selection of pure vegetarian restaurants. Most restaurants listed are in the downtown area, off or near Zion Square and the Ben Yehuda Pedestrian Mall. May the spiritual grace of the food you eat combine with the other spiritual aspects of your visit for a special and unique stay in this special city!

Alumah ✿

8 Ya'avetz Street   **(02) 255-014**
(next to the Bell Center)

Dairy. All organic products. Has a stone mill on premises to grind fresh wheat, rye, and barley flour. Makes sourdough bread and rye products. Indoor and garden seating. Uses no aluminum or teflon pans -- only stainless steel, ceramic or glass. Takeout store is next to the restaurant. Menu includes quiche, vegetable pies, combination plates, and the *Alumah Special* -- fresh mushrooms, tempeh, vegetables, and almonds sautéed in olive oil and tamari served over rice. Assortment of natural fruit juices, soy shakes, herbal teas, and organic grape juice. Tempeh made on premises, and the falafel is prepared without oil! Serves fish. **Hours: Sunday - Thursday: 10:00 AM - 11:00 PM, Friday: 10:00 AM - 2:00 PM, Saturday: Closed. Meals Served: Breakfast, Lunch, & Dinner. Glatt Kosher. VISA/MasterCard/American Express. Average Price (Main Course): 20 NIS ($6.50).**

✿ - Recommended Restaurant

Beit Ticho "Nifgashim" ✡

9 HaRav Kook Street   **(02) 244-186**

Dairy. A Jerusalem landmark, situated in a museum which was the home
of well-known eye doctor Avraham Ticho and his artist-wife Anna, whose
works are on display. Indoor seating/quiet garden with much greenery.
Menu includes soups, salads, stuffed potatoes, stuffed vegetables, and
desserts. **Hours: Sunday - Thursday: 10:00 AM - 12:00 AM (midnight), Friday: 10:00 AM - 2:45 PM, Saturday Evening: Until 12:00
AM (midnight). Meals Served: Breakfast, Lunch, & Dinner. Kosher.
Traveler's Checks accepted. Average Price (Main Course): 18 NIS
($6).**

B'Sograim

45 Ussishkin Street (in Rehavia neighborhood)   (02) 245-333

Dairy. Located in an historic building in Jerusalem's Rehavia neighborhood, a few minutes from the city center. On Friday afternoons
B'Sograim turns into a favorite 'hang out' for Israeli journalists and
television personalities. Menu includes soups, salads, vegetable pies,
pastas, and desserts. **Hours: Sunday - Thursday: 9:00 AM - 12:00 AM
(midnight), Friday: 9:00 AM - 3:00 PM, Saturday Evening: 8:00 PM -
12:00 AM (midnight). Meals Served: Breakfast, Lunch, & Dinner.
Kosher. Reservations preferred. Traveler's Checks & Foreign
Currency accepted. Average Price (Main Course): 24 NIS ($8).**

Cheesecake

23 Yoel Solomon Street   **(02) 245-082**
(Nahalat Shiva Pedestrian Mall)

Dairy. Frequented by the local English speaking community, including
tourists and students studying on overseas programs. Menu includes
soups, stuffed potatoes, salads, vegetarian chili, and sandwiches.
Breakfast is served only on Friday mornings with an extensive menu.
Well-known for their cheesecake, made with a special recipe and over 30
flavors. **Hours: Sunday - Thursday: 10:30 AM - 12:00 AM (midnight),
Friday: 9:30 AM - one hour before sundown, Saturday Evening: Until
1:00 AM. Meals Served: Breakfast, Lunch, & Dinner. Kosher.
Smoking Area. VISA/American Express. Traveler's Checks & Foreign Currency accepted. Average Price (Main Course): 18 NIS ($6).**

✡ - Recommended Restaurant

Etnachta

12 Yoel Solomon Street   **(02) 256-584**
(Nahalat Shiva Pedestrian Mall)

Italian. Located in a 110-year-old building which was the local Nahalat Shiva bakery. Indoor/outdoor seating. Menu includes salads, stuffed potatoes, quiche, pasta, pancakes, crepes, and desserts. **Hours: Sunday - Thursday: 7:30 AM - 1:00 AM, Friday: 7:30 AM - one hour before sundown, Saturday Evening: Until 1:00 AM. Meals Served: Breakfast, Lunch, & Dinner. Kosher. VISA/MasterCard. Traveler's Checks & Foreign Currency accepted. Average Price (Main Course): 18 NIS ($6).**

Four Seasons

54 Haneviim Street   **(02) 252-195**

Dairy. Situated in an historic building which used to serve as an arms warehouse for the pre-state *Haganah* army. Located on the border of Jerusalem's religious neighborhood of Meah Shearim. Large dining area and patio, pleasant atmosphere. Menu includes soups, salads, quiche, pasta, omelettes, special main courses, and desserts. **Hours: Sunday - Thursday: 9:00 AM - 12:00 AM (midnight), Friday: 9:00 AM - 3:00 PM, Saturday Evening: Until 12:00 AM (midnight). Meals Served: Breakfast, Lunch, & Dinner. Kosher. No smoking on premises. VISA/MasterCard. Traveler's Checks & Foreign Currency accepted. Average Price (Main Course): 21 NIS ($7).**

Kohinoor

Jerusalem Holiday Inn, Givat Ram   **(02) 581-367**

This is the *kosher version* of the Tandoori Indian restaurant chain, with full kosher certification. For full description, please see the listing for *Tandoori* in Tel Aviv.

La Pasta

16 Yosef Rivlin Street   (02) 257-687
(Nahalat Shiva Pedestrian Mall, 2nd Floor)

Italian. Elegant, large dining area. Menu includes pasta, hot and cold vegetable appetizers, soups, and desserts. Eggless pasta can be ordered. **Hours: Sunday - Thursday: 12:00 PM (noon) - 3:00 PM and 5:30 PM - 11:30 PM, Friday: 12:00 PM (noon) - one hour before sundown, Saturday Evening: Until 11:30 PM. Meals Served: Lunch & Dinner. Kosher. Reservations preferred. VISA/MasterCard/American Express. Traveler's Checks & Foreign Currency accepted. Average Price (Main Course): 27 NIS ($9).**

La Riviera

4 Dorot Rishonim Street   (02) 248-347
(Ben Yehuda Pedestrian Mall)

Italian. Interior is designed as a European street -- complete with pavement floors, a street light, water gutters, and window shutters. Each table has a questionnaire which allows diners to create their own salad or breakfast. In the summertime, you can sit outside among the large crowds and "people watch" the Ben Yehuda street crowd. Menu includes soups, salads, baguette and croissant sandwiches, toasts, omelettes, pizza, crepes, and desserts. **Hours: Sunday - Thursday: 7:00 AM - 12:00 AM (midnight), Friday: 8:00 AM - one hour before sundown, Saturday Evening: Until 12:00 AM (midnight). Meals Served: Breakfast, Lunch, & Dinner. Kosher. VISA/MasterCard/Diner's/ American Express. Traveler's Checks & Foreign Currency accepted. Average Price (Main Course): 21 NIS ($7).**

Le Tsriff

26 King David Street (at the YMCA)   (02) 246-521

Mixed. Designed by the architect of the Empire State Building, the YMCA is a city landmark. Outside seating overlooks twelve cypress trees that represent the 12 disciples of Jesus, 12 tribes of Israel, and 12 companions of Mohammed. Menu includes soups, salads, vegetable pies, sandwiches, and desserts. **Hours: 8:00 AM - 12:00 AM (midnight), Daily. Meals Served: Breakfast, Lunch, & Dinner. Reservations preferred. VISA/MasterCard/American Express/Diner's. Foreign Currency accepted. Average Price (Main Course): 21 NIS ($7).**

Little Italy

38 Keren Hayesod Street   (02) 617-638
(near Laromme Hotel)

Italian. Nice atmosphere. Menu includes salads, pizza, spaghetti, fettucini, ravioli, baked ziti, lasagna (vegetable & spinach), and desserts. **Hours: Sunday - Thursday: 10:00 AM - 12:00 AM (midnight), Friday: 10:00 AM - 4:00 PM, Saturday Evening: Until 12:00 AM (midnight). Meals Served: Lunch & Dinner. Kosher. Smoking Area. Reservations preferred. VISA/MasterCard/American Express/Diner's. Traveler's Checks & Foreign Currency accepted. Average Price (Main Course): 30 NIS ($10).**

Luigi

12 Yoel Solomon Street   (02) 232-524
(Nahalat Shiva Pedestrian Mall)

Italian. Outside seating on Nahalat Shiva Pedestrian Mall. Italian background music. Menu includes pasta, pizza, antipastos, and salads. **Hours: Sunday - Thursday: 8:00 AM - 12:00 AM (midnight), Friday: 8:00 AM - 3:00 PM, Saturday Evening: Until 12:45 AM. Meals Served: Breakfast, Lunch, & Dinner. Kosher. Traveler's Checks & Foreign Currency accepted. Average Price (Main Course): 21 NIS ($7).**

The Macrobiotic Center in Israel

1 Ben Maimon Avenue   (02) 636-223/636-256
(corner Gaza Street in Rehavia neighborhood)

Macrobiotic. Some organic products used. Menu includes soups, grains, proteins, cooked vegetables, salads, and desserts. Menu changes daily. Uses organic vegetables. **Hours: Sunday - Thursday: 12:30 PM - 3:30 PM, Friday & Saturday: Closed. Meals Served: Lunch only. Kosher. VISA/MasterCard. Traveler's Checks & Foreign Currency accepted. Average Price (Main Course): 21 NIS ($7).**

Magritte

9 Yoel Solomon)   (02) 234-499
(alleyway of Nahalat Shiva Pedestrian Mall)

Dairy. The restaurant's motif is based on the French surrealistic painter
Magritte. Inside/outside seating. Menu includes soups, salads, quiche,
cakes, desserts, plus a *Surrealistic Salad* (mushrooms, celery, kiwi, and
avocado). **Hours: Sunday - Thursday: 9:30 AM - 12:00 AM
(midnight), Friday: 9:30 AM - one hour before sundown, Saturday
Evening: Until 12:00 AM (midnight). Meals Served: Breakfast,
Lunch, & Dinner. Kosher. Smoking Area. Foreign Currency
accepted. Average Price (Main Course): 17 NIS ($5.50).**

Makom Balev

18 King George Street   (02) 250-333
(Lev Yerushaliym Hotel -- 1st Floor)

Dairy. Menu includes soups, salads, pies, blintzes, pasta, and desserts.
**Hours: Sunday - Thursday: 7:00 AM - 11:00 PM, Friday: 7:00 AM-
2:00 PM, Saturday Evening: Until 11:00 PM. Meals Served: Breakfast, Lunch, & Dinner. Glatt Kosher. Smoking Area. Reservations
preferred. VISA/MasterCard/Diner's/American Express. Traveler's
Checks & Foreign Currency accepted. Average Price (Main Course):
27 NIS ($9).**

Mamma Mia

38 King George Street   (02) 248-080

Italian. Located in one of the first buildings outside of the old city
(1899) which is now a beautifully renovated Jerusalem townhouse.
Menu includes homemade pasta and bread (focallia). Serves a fresh fruit
ice cream. **Hours: Sunday - Thursday: 12:00 PM (noon) - 12:00 AM
(midnight), Friday: 12:00 PM (noon) - one hour before sundown,
Saturday Evening: Until 12:00 AM (midnight). Meals Served:
Breakfast, Lunch, & Dinner. Kosher. Smoking Area. VISA/
MasterCard/Diner's/American Express/Eurocard. Traveler's Checks
& Foreign Currency accepted. Average Price (Main Course): 24 NIS
($8).**

The Natural Choice

Jaffa Street 136   **(02) 389-539**
(near Mahane Yehuda Market)

Bakery. Baked goods made from natural flours - whole wheat and
organic. No eggs or preservatives.

Of Course!

Emile Bohta Street-Yemin Moshe   **(02) 244-585**
(in Zionist Confederation House)

Dairy. Some organic products used. Situated in a building dating back
to the 5th Century, which was an old age home, Byzantine house of
prayer, Crusader monastery, and Greek church. Spectacular view of Old
City facing Mount Zion and David's Tower. Pleasant, eclectic atmos-
phere. Menu includes soups, salads, stuffed vegetables, quiche, daily
specials, and desserts. **Hours: Sunday - Thursday: 11:00 AM - 11:00
PM, Friday: 11:00 AM - 2:00 PM, Saturday Evening: Until 11:00 PM.
Meals Served: Lunch & Dinner. Kosher. Reservations preferred.
VISA/MasterCard/American Express. Traveler's Checks & Foreign
Currency accepted. Average Price (Main Course): 21 NIS ($7).**

Off The Square

6 Yoel Solomon Street   **(02) 242-549**
(Nahalat Shiva Pedestrian Mall)

Dairy. **Hours: Sunday - Thursday: 9:00 AM - 12:00 AM (midnight),
Friday: 9:00 AM - one hour before sundown, Saturday Evening: Until
1:00 AM. Meals Served: Breakfast, Lunch, & Dinner. Glatt Kosher.
Smoking Area. VISA/MasterCard/Diner's/American Express.
Traveler's Checks & Foreign Currency accepted. Average Price
(Main Course): 25 NIS ($8.50).**

Pera E Mela

7 HaMa'alot Street   (02) 251-975

Italian. Quaint Italian restaurant, with limited indoor and outdoor seating. Menu includes soups, salads, pasta, pizza, baked potatoes, crepes, and desserts. **Hours: Sunday - Thursday: 11:00 AM - 12:00 AM (midnight), Friday: 10:00 AM - 3:00 PM, Saturday Evening: Until 1:00 AM. Meals Served: Lunch & Dinner. Kosher. VISA/MasterCard/ American Express/EuroCard. Average Price (Main Course): 21 NIS ($7).**

Primavera

**47 King George Street   (02) 259-111
(at the Plaza Hotel)**

Italian. Elegant atmosphere. Menu includes soups, pasta, and antipastos. **Hours: Sunday - Thursday: 12:30 PM - 3:00 PM and 6:30 PM - 11:00 PM, Friday: Closed, Saturday Evening: Until 11:00 PM. Meals Served: Lunch & Dinner. Kosher. Smoking Area. Reservations preferred. VISA/MasterCard/American Express/Diner's. Traveler's Checks & Foreign Currency accepted. Average Price (Main Course): 30 NIS ($10).**

Rimon Cafe

**4 Luntz Street   (02) 243-746
(Ben Yehuda Pedestrian Mall)**

Dairy. One of the most popular and bustling cafes in Jerusalem. Favorite hangout for university students and tourists. Plenty of seating inside and outside. Menu includes soups, salads, sandwiches, toasts, omelettes, stuffed potatoes, spaghetti, pizza, blintzes (sweet and main course), soy schnitzel, and vegetable patty platters. Large assortment of desserts. **Hours: Sunday - Thursday: 7:00 AM - 12:00 AM (midnight), Friday: 7:00 AM - one hour before sundown, Saturday Evening: Until 12:00 AM (midnight). Meals Served: Breakfast, Lunch, & Dinner. Kosher. Smoking Area. VISA/MasterCard/Diner's/American Express. Traveler's Checks & Foreign Currency accepted. Average Price (Main Course): 15 NIS ($5).**

Roquefort

12 Yoel Solomon Street   **(02) 234-649**
(Nahalat Shiva Pedestrian Mall)

Dairy. Run by the Bumgartens, a veteran Jerusalem family whose previous family business was in the same location for the past 53 years. Menu includes soups, salads, toasts, pizza, vegetable pies, stuffed potatoes, pasta, and desserts. **Hours: Sunday - Thursday: 7:00 AM - 2:00 AM, Friday: 7:00 AM - one hour before sundown, Saturday Evening: Until 2:00 AM. Meals Served: Breakfast, Lunch, & Dinner. Kosher. VISA/ MasterCard/American Express/Diner's. Traveler's Checks & Foreign Currency accepted. Average Price (Main Course): 21 NIS ($7).**

Rosemary ✿

28 King David Street (near King David Hotel)   **(02) 258-157**

Dairy. Some organic products are used. Quiet, pleasant dining atmosphere. Indoor/garden seating. Tourist crowd from the local hotels. Menu includes soups, salads, toasts, vegetable pies, quiche, pizza, pasta, and desserts. Will prepare vegan meals if ordered in advance. **Hours: Sunday - Thursday: 8:00 AM - 12:30 AM, Friday: 8:00 AM - one hour before sundown, Saturday Evening: Until 1:30 AM. Meals Served: Breakfast, Lunch, & Dinner. Kosher. Reservations preferred. VISA/Diner's. Traveler's Checks & Foreign Currency accepted. Average Price (Main Course): 21 NIS ($7).**

The 7th Place

37 Hillel Street (Beit Agron Building)   **(02) 254-495**

Indian/Israeli. Located in the center for foreign journalists, Beit Agron. As Israel has the largest concentration of foreign journalists in the world, it is not too difficult to find! Live entertainment on Tuesday, Thursday, and Saturday. Menu includes soups, toasts, vegetable pies, blintzes, Indian dishes (mostly vegan), and eggplant, hummus, and Oriental salad. **Hours: Sunday - Thursday: 8:00 AM - 12:00 AM (midnight), Friday: 8:00 AM - one hour before sundown, Saturday Evening: Until 1:00 AM. Meals Served: Breakfast, Lunch, & Dinner. Kosher. Smoking Area. Reservations preferred. VISA/MasterCard. Traveler's Checks & Foreign Currency accepted. Average Price (Main Course): 21 NIS ($7).**

✿ - Recommended Restaurant

Sheba

Located in a Lane between   (02) 249-138
63 Jaffa Road & 8 Agrippas Street

Ethiopian. Some organic products used. Food is prepared by Ethiopian immigrants according to traditional cooking techniques, using sauces called *wats* and eaten in communal platter dishes using *injera* -- Ethiopian bread. They will prepare a full vegetarian menu for visiting groups. Menu includes soups, vegetable entrée (potatoes in spicy sauce, Ethiopian hummus), and desserts. **Hours: Sunday - Thursday: 11:30 AM - 3:00 PM and 6:00 PM - 11:00 PM, Friday: Closed, Saturday Evening: 7:30 PM - 11:00 PM. Meals Served: Lunch & Dinner. Kosher. Smoking Area. Reservations preferred. Traveler's Checks & Foreign Currency accepted. Average Price (Main Course): 25 NIS ($8.50).**

"Ta'am Hameshek" Bakery

17 Bezalel Street   (02) 246-536

Bakery. Freshly baked cakes and cookies made with organic ingredients. **Hours: Sunday - Thursday: 8:00 AM - 4:00 PM.**

Tavlin

16 Yoel Solomon Street   (02) 243-847
(Nahalat Shivat Pedestrian Mall)

Dairy. A well-known Jerusalem establishment for over 10 years. Popular with local Israeli crowd and visitors. Inside/outside seating on Yoel Solomon street. Menu includes soups, salads, crepes, vegetable pies, omelettes, and desserts. **Hours: Sunday - Thursday: 8:00 AM - 12:30 AM, Friday: 8:00 AM - 4:00 PM, Saturday Evening: Until 12:30 PM. Meals Served: Breakfast, Lunch, & Dinner. Kosher. Traveler's Checks & Foreign Currency accepted. Average Price (Main Course): 21 NIS ($7).**

Te 'enim Vegetarian Cuisine ✡

21 Emek Refaim Street
(German Colony Neighborhood)

(02) 630-048

Vegetarian/Ethnic. A splendid restaurant located in the quaint German Colony neighborhood. *Te'enim's* owner, Patrick, is of Algerian and French descent, and he places an emphasis on style and cuisine for his vegetarian dishes. There is a careful balance between vegetarian and vegan main and side dishes. From 8:00 AM - 11:00 AM is a breakfast buffet for the price of 22 NIS ($7.50). Menu includes soups (miso, seaweed), salads (tabuli, Chinese, green), sandwiches, vegan vegetable pie, skewered tofu, mushrooms, and vegetables marinated in red wine, plus daily specials and natural juices. **Hours: Sunday - Thursday: 8:00 AM - 11:00 PM, Friday: 8:00 AM - 3:30 PM, Saturday Evening: Closed. Meals Served: Breakfast, Lunch, & Dinner. Kosher. Foreign Currency accepted. No smoking on premises. Average Price (Main Course) 15 NIS ($5).**

Valentino's

Hyatt Hotel
(Near Hebrew University)

(02) 331-234

Italian (Northern). Intimate, elegant atmosphere. Special attentive service. Menu includes soups, salads, pasta, and vegetable side dishes. **Hours: Sunday - Thursday: 6:30 PM - 11:30 PM, Friday: Closed, Saturday Evening: Until 11:00 PM. Meals Served: Dinner only. Kosher. Smoking Area. Reservations preferred. VISA/MasterCard/ Diner's/American Express. Traveler's Checks & Foreign Currency accepted. Average Price (Main Course): 25 NIS ($8.50).**

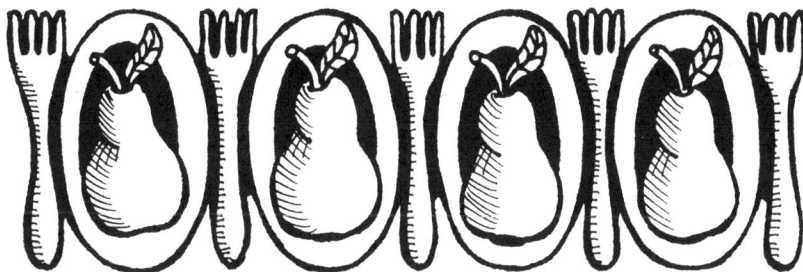

✡ - Recommended Restaurant

Village Green. ✡

Self Service Restaurant: 10 Ben Yehuda Street
(Pedestrian Mall)   **(02) 252-007**
Full Service Restaurant: 1 Bezalel Street   **(02) 251-464**

Vegetarian. Some organic products used. **The only pure vegetarian restaurant in downtown Jerusalem.** Run by Barry Sibul, a long time veteran of the Jerusalem health food business. Favorite meeting place of the vegetarian community in Jerusalem. The self-service restaurant can be a bit cramped when waiting to order food, so patience and good humor are required!! A full service restaurant has opened at the Bezalel Academy of Arts and Designs with same delicious menu, plus a breakfast buffet from 8:00 AM - 11:00 AM. Make sure you use the entrance on Bezalel street. Menu includes vegetable pies, grains, vegetables, and salads. Changes daily. Also caters vegetarian weddings, Bar-Mitzvahs, and other occasions. **Hours (same at both locations): Sunday - Thursday: 8:00 AM - 10:00 PM, Friday: 11:00 AM - one hour before sundown, Saturday Evening: Closed. Meals Served: Lunch & Dinner. Kosher. No smoking on premises. VISA/MasterCard/ Diner's. Foreign Currency accepted. Average Price (Main Course): 21 NIS ($7).**

Ye Olde English Tea Room ✡

68 Jaffa Street/58 Haneviim Street   **(02) 233-853**
(in Habustan Building)

Dairy. Located in the 200 year old *Bustan* building, home of a well-known Jerusalem artist who makes wooden *dreidels* (spinning tops) for Hanukkah -- from the traditional to Mickey Mouse! The *Tea Room* has a lovely British atmosphere and pleasant service. A harpist plays in the evenings. Menu includes soups, sandwiches, Welsh rarebit, full dessert menu, and of course -- English Tea!! **Hours: Sunday - Thursday: 8:30 AM - 11:00 PM, Friday: 8:30 AM - 3:00 PM, Saturday Evening: Until 12:00 AM (midnight). Meals Served: Breakfast, Lunch, & Dinner. Kosher. Smoking Area. VISA/MasterCard. Foreign Currency accepted. Average Entree Price: 15 NIS ($5).**

✡ - Recommended Restaurant

Tel Aviv

Tel Aviv advertises itself as the "city that never rests." It really is true! You can go out at any time of the day or night in Tel Aviv and see people walking on the streets in all corners of the city. Some visitors find this is exciting, while others find it too much like home and prefer a quieter atmosphere. There is no doubt that Tel Aviv has much to offer and is the social and economic heartbeat of the country.

Tel Aviv is a beach city, and referred to in terms of "North" and "South." The main roads which traverse Tel Aviv where many restaurants are located include Hayarkon Street, Allenby Street (which becomes Ben Yehuda Street), and Dizengoff Street. These are the main areas in Tel Aviv where restaurants are found:

Nahalat Binyamin -- A pedestrian mall near the Carmel Market and off Allenby Street.

Shenkin Street -- A block north of Nahalat Binyamin. A very "in" area where artists, students, and other interesting personalities live and frequent.

Dizengoff Center -- At the intersection of Dizengoff and King George Streets. Large indoor shopping mall.

Habima -- Home of the Israeli theater and philharmonic orchestra. Bordering Dizengoff near Ibn Gvirol Street (east of Dizengoff Center).

Tel Aviv Promenade -- The beach front, joining HaYarkon street at Gordon Street.

Dizengoff Circle -- North of Dizengoff Center, where the statue by the famous Israeli artist, Agam is located.

North Dizengoff -- Upscale part of town with fancy shops and restaurants.

North Tel Aviv -- Yehuda Macabbi Street and North Ibn Gvirol Street. Upscale and popular with the "yuppie" Tel Aviv set.

Alexander ✡

81 Yehuda HaMaccabi Street   **(03) 605-8910**
(North Tel Aviv)

Mixed. Some organic products served. Considered Israel's #1 coffee house, it is the favorite spot of Israel's elite -- Mrs. Rabin, government ministers, famous actors, and business magnates all can be seen here. Excellent service, large indoor/outdoor seating. Menu includes soups, sandwiches, a vegetable combination plate, omelettes, stuffed potatoes, pasta, and desserts. A vegetarian combination plate of various vegetable choices of the day. The cook informed me that they use organic lettuce. **Hours: 7:00 AM - 1:00 AM, Daily. Meals Served: Breakfast, Lunch, & Dinner. Smoking Area. VISA/MasterCard/Diner's. Foreign Currency accepted. Average Price (Main Course): 23 NIS ($7.50).**

Alexander

22 Rambam Street   **(03) 510-0571**
(Nahalat Binyamin Pedestrian Mall)

Mixed. A very "in" restaurant that attracts an upscale, yuppie crowd. Avant garde decor, with seating inside and on the pedestrian mall. Menu includes soups, vegetables, casseroles, salads, pasta, and desserts. **Hours: Sunday - Thursday: 9:00 AM - 12:00 AM (midnight), Friday: 8:30 AM - 2:00 AM, Saturday: 10:00 AM - 12:00 AM (midnight). Meals Served: Breakfast, Lunch, & Dinner. Smoking Area. Reservations preferred. VISA/MasterCard/Diner's. Average Price (Main Course): 25 NIS ($8.50).**

✡ - Recommended Restaurant

America

1 Daniel Frisch Street   **(03) 695-0721**
(ZOA House)

American. If you have been on vacation a bit too long and might be long-
ing for "home," then America is the place to go. Located in a building
established by the Zionist Organization of America, this restaurant features pictures of various U.S. cities and a New York City subway map on
the walls! Plenty of seating both inside and outside. Menu includes
pasta, pizza, salads, vegetable pies, omelettes, desserts, and a varied
drink/spirit list. **Hours: 24 hours a day, every day of the week! Meals
Served: Breakfast, Lunch, & Dinner. Smoking Area. VISA/
MasterCard/Diner's/American Express. Traveler's Checks accepted.
Average Price (Main Course): 24 NIS ($8).**

Apropro

Tarsat 4A Heichal Hatarbut   **(03) 528-9288/9**
(Habima Theater)

Dairy. Clientele is upscale (age 30+) including VIP's, Knesset Members,
and members of the business community. Elegant, black decor. Pianists
in the evenings from 8:00 PM. Menu includes salads, omelettes, sandwiches and toasts, pasta, crepes, desserts, and spirit menu. There is a
special Thai menu consisting of vegetable and noodle dishes, some
vegan. **Hours: Sunday - Thursday: 8:30 AM - 12:00 AM (midnight),
Friday: 8:30 AM - 1:30 AM, Saturday: 6:00 AM - 12:30 AM. Meals
Served: Breakfast, Lunch, & Dinner. Smoking Area. Reservations
preferred. VISA/MasterCard/American Express/Diner's. Traveler's
Checks & Foreign Currency accepted. Average Price (Main Course):
26 NIS ($8.50).**

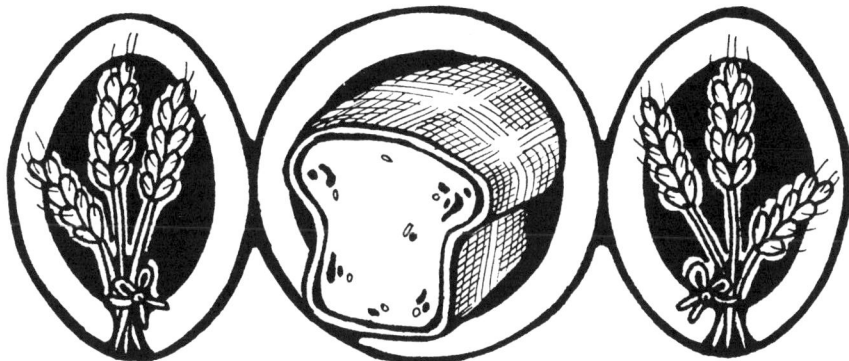

Asia House Restaurant

4 Weizman Street   (03) 691-0717
(near the law court)

Dairy. Some organic products used. Located in Asia House, a well-known office complex in Tel Aviv which houses many foreign embassies, businesses, and law offices. Lunch with diplomats and the Tel Aviv business elite. Menu includes sandwiches, omelettes, soups, salads, crepes, stuffed potatoes, blintzes, and desserts. **Hours: Sunday - Thursday: 7:30 AM - 5:00 PM, Friday: 7:30 AM - 2:00 PM, Saturday: Closed. Meals Served: Breakfast & Lunch. Kosher. Smoking Area. VISA/MasterCard/American Express/Diners. Traveler's Checks & Foreign Currency accepted. Average Price (Main Course): 25 NIS ($8.50).**

Back To Nature

90 Frishman Street   (03) 534-4422
(corner of Massryk Street,
across from the Tel Aviv Municipal Building)

Vegetarian. All organic products used. As the name implies, this restaurant has a very earthy atmosphere. The menu is certainly a delight for any vegetarian, as they offer veggie and vegan dishes. The service is a bit slow and staff not very accommodating. Menu includes soups, salads, vegetable pies, stuffed vegetables, eggplant "chopped liver," grains, natural juices, shakes, and a dessert menu. No fried foods. **Hours: Sunday - Thursday: 10:00 AM - 11:00 PM, Friday: 10:00 AM - 4:00 PM, Saturday Evening: Until 11:00 PM. Meals Served: Breakfast, Lunch, & Dinner. Kosher. No smoking on premises. VISA/MasterCard/Diner's/American Express. Average Price (Main Course): 11 NIS ($3.50).**

Cafe Afrsemon

230 Dizengoff Street   (03) 524-2425
(North Dizengoff near Jabotinsky Street)

Dairy/Israeli. Small local cafe. Menu includes salads, omelettes, vegetable pies, blintzes, toasts, and desserts. They also have Middle Eastern Food such as *techina*, hummus, *majdara* (lentils and rice), and *malawach* (fried dough). **Hours: Sunday - Thursday: 8:00 AM - 8:00 PM, Friday: 8:00 AM - one hour before sundown, Saturday Evening: Until 12:00 AM (midnight). Meals Served: Breakfast, Lunch, & Dinner. Kosher. Smoking Area. VISA/MasterCard. Foreign Currency accepted. Average Price (Main Course): 15 NIS ($5).**

Cafe Blue

4 Yehuda HaMaccabi Street   (03) 604-2489
(North Tel Aviv)

Mixed. Upscale, hip crowd, 25 - 35 year-olds in evenings. Menu includes soups, salads, sandwiches, stuffed potatoes, pasta, fruits, and desserts. **Hours: Sunday - Thursday, Friday: 7:00 AM - 1:00 AM, Saturday: 9:00 AM - 1:00 AM. Meals Served: Breakfast, Lunch, & Dinner. VISA/MasterCard/Diner's. Traveler's Checks accepted. Average Price (Main Course): 18 NIS ($6).**

Cafe De La Paix

290 Dizengoff Street   (03) 604-0081
(North Dizengoff)

Mixed. On the walls are sketched pastel copies of Toulouse Lautrec's artwork drawn by an Israeli art student. The pastels are so close to the originals that, perhaps, Lautrec's ghost may be working here! Attractive, interior with wood floors and hanging plants. Upscale crowd. Indoor/outdoor seating. Menu includes soups, salads, toasts, quiche, vegetable pies, vegetable dishes, and desserts. Vegan dishes include stir-fried veggies and hot mushroom salad. **Hours: 8:00 AM - 2:00 AM, Daily. Meals Served: Breakfast, Lunch, & Dinner. Smoking Area. VISA/MasterCard/Diner's. Foreign Currency accepted. Average Price (Main Course): 21 NIS ($7).**

Cafe Kazze ✿
19 Shenkin Street   **(03) 293-756**

Dairy. Cafe Kazze is located in a four room apartment which allows for a spacious, yet intimate setting. Crowd is pleasant, artsy in their late 20's through early 40's. In the back is a large, private garden. Friendly staff. Menu includes salads, a walnut paté, banana bread, quiche, spaghetti, and desserts. **Hours: Sunday - Thursday: 8:00 AM - 12:00 AM (midnight), Friday: 8:00 AM - 3:30 PM, Saturday: Closed. Meals Served: Breakfast, Lunch, & Dinner. Kosher. Smoking Area. Average Price (Main Course): 19 NIS ($6.50).**

Cafe London
Dizengoff Center (Gate 3)   **(03) 203-707**

Dairy. Pianist on Monday, Wednesday, and Friday nights. Menu includes soups, salad bar, toasts, croissants, omelettes, baked potatoes, pasta, pancakes, sweet crepes, fruit, and desserts. **Hours: Sunday - Thursday: 8:00 AM - 11:00 PM, Friday: 7:30 AM - 4:00 PM, Saturday: 8:00 AM - 11:00 PM. Meals Served: Breakfast, Lunch, & Dinner. Smoking Area. VISA/MasterCard/American Express/Diner's. Traveler's Checks & Foreign Currency accepted. Average Price (Main Course): 21 NIS ($7).**

Cafe Nordau
145 Ben Yehuda Street   **(03) 524-0007**

Mixed. Ecologically-minded owners -- with signs in the windows supporting Israel's ban on mistreatment of dolphins, and menus printed on recycled paper. There is also a separate menu for dogs, who can eat free at the restaurant. One positive outcome of my visit to *Cafe Nordau* is that the manager expressed an interest in ordering organic vegetables, and making a connection between them and the Israel Organic Farmer's Association. Indoor/outdoor seating, pleasant atmosphere. Menu includes soups, salads, quiche, stuffed potatoes, toasts, pasta, and desserts. The menu features a forest mushroom schnitzel. **Hours: Sunday - Friday: 8:00 AM - 1:00 AM, Saturday: 10:00 AM - 1:00 AM. Meals Served: Breakfast, Lunch, & Dinner. Smoking Area. VISA/ MasterCard/Diner's/American Express. Traveler's Checks & Foreign Currency accepted. Average Price (Main Course): 21 NIS ($7).**

✿ - Recommended Restaurant

Cafe Nouveau

148 Ben Yehuda Street   (03) 524-8818

Mixed. In the evenings, there is live Brazilian and jazz music. Menu includes soups, salads, quiche, vegetable pies, pasta, and spirits. **Hours: 9:00 AM - 1:00 AM, Daily. Meals Served: Breakfast, Lunch, & Dinner. VISA/MasterCard/Diner's. Foreign Currency accepted. Average Price (Main Course): 21 NIS ($7).**

Cafe Pinati

106 Dizengoff Street   (03) 523-8257
(near Frishman Street)

Dairy. A 60 year old local Tel Aviv cafe that has undergone quite an extensive facelift! Indoor/outdoor seating. Menu includes soups, salads, omelettes, toasts, sandwiches, blintzes, pasta, Chinese vegetables, and desserts. **Hours: Sunday - Thursday: 7:30 AM - 1:00 AM, Friday: 7:30 AM - 3:00 AM, Saturday: 7:30 AM - 2:00 AM. Meals Served: Breakfast, Lunch, & Dinner. VISA/MasterCard/Diner's/American Express. Foreign Currency accepted. Average Price (Main Course): 17 NIS ($6.50).**

Cafe Rowal

111 Dizengoff Street, 1st Floor   (03) 524-3410
(near Frishman Street)

Mixed. 30 years ago, *Cafe Rowal* was the #1 coffee house in Tel Aviv frequented by the local bohemian crowd. Today it is a meeting place during the day for bridge clubs (the tables are bridge tables) with entertainment on Friday and Saturday nights. Indoor/Outdoor seating. Menu includes soups, salads, toasts, quiche, blintzes, stuffed potatoes, stuffed vegetables, pasta, desserts, and spirits. **Hours: Sunday - Thursday: 10:00 AM - 12:30 AM, Friday: 10:00 AM - 3:00 AM, Saturday Evening: Until 1:00 AM. Meals Served: Breakfast, Lunch, & Dinner. Reservations preferred. VISA/MasterCard. Average Price (Main Course): 18 NIS ($6).**

Cafe Tamar ✡
57 Shenkin Street
(03) 562-2376

Dairy. A bit of Tel Aviv nostalgia, *Cafe Tamar* achieved overnight success after a famous Israeli radio hit a few years ago featured its name in the song. The owner, Sara Stern, can be seen at the cash register ringing up an art student's bill while at the same time offering tips on how to find an apartment in the area. Take a newspaper from the bin and enjoy a drink, while mingling among the local crowd of hip young students and artists. A true Tel Aviv experience!! There isn't a menu, but they do serve Yemenite toasts and salad in addition to coffee and cakes. **Hours: Sunday - Thursday: 7:00 AM - 8:00 PM, Friday: 7:00 AM - 7:00 PM, Saturday: Closed. Meals Served: Breakfast & Lunch. Smoking Area.**

Cafe Zoo
57 Yehudah HaMaccabi Street
(North Tel Aviv)
(03) 605-5022

Mixed. The crowd at this *Zoo* located on the chic section of Northern Tel Aviv is upscale society people during the day, and at night a younger "Yuppie" crowd. Indoor/outdoor seating. Menu includes salads, sandwiches, pasta, stir-fried Chinese vegetables, Asian noodles (can be ordered as a veggie dish), stuffed potatoes, fruit, and desserts. **Hours: 8:00 AM - 1:00 AM, Daily. Meals Served: Breakfast, Lunch, & Dinner. Smoking Area. VISA/MasterCard/Diner's. Average Price (Main Course): 24 NIS ($8).**

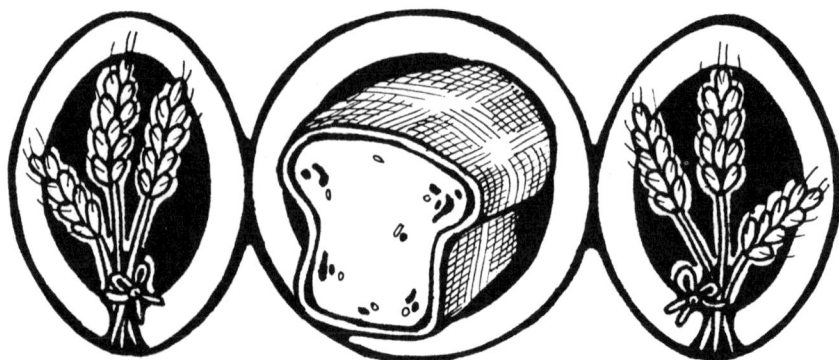

✡ - Recommended Restaurant

Eternity
60 Ben Yehuda Street   **(03) 203-151**

Vegan Soul Food. All organic products used. Restaurant started by the Hebrew Israelite Community of Dimona (Black Hebrews) in Southern Israel who also run a similar restaurant in Chicago, Illinois. All food is made on the premises with natural ingredients (whole wheat gluten and soybean products). Simple appearance. Menu includes wheat burgers, tofu filet, vege-schnitzel, bar-b-que twist, and okara sticks, all of which can be ordered either as a main dish or sandwich. They have a selection of salads and soups, plus home-made tofu ice cream for dessert. **Hours: Sunday - Thursday: 9:00 AM - 11:00 PM, Friday: 9:00 AM - 2:00 PM, Saturday Evening: Until 11:00 PM. Meals Served: Breakfast, Lunch, & Dinner. Kosher. No smoking on premises. Average Price (Main Course): 18 NIS ($6).**

Goldstein's Deli Nosh
Dizengoff Center(Gate #3)   **(03) 296-056**

Dairy. Family restaurant run by Mrs. Goldstein, with a "hamish" atmosphere. Mr.Goldstein was chief chef for the Israel Dan Hotels chain until retiring, but he claims that Mrs. Goldstein is responsible for the kitchen!! Menu includes soups, salads, omelettes, crepes, sandwiches, cakes, and fruit juices. **Hours: Sunday - Thursday: 8:00 AM - 9:00 PM, Friday: 8:00 AM - 4:00 PM, Saturday Evening: Until 12:00 AM (midnight). Meals Served: Breakfast, Lunch, & Dinner. Kosher. VISA/MasterCard/Diner's. Average Price (Main Course): 13 NIS ($4.50).**

The Green Corner
80 Rockach Boulevard   **(03) 493-441**
(at the Center for a Beautiful Israel-North Hayarkon Park)

Dairy. Situated in the Center for a Beautiful Israel which runs educational programs about nature and the land of Israel. A quiet respite from the big city, with a view of greenery and running water. Menu includes soups, salads, sandwiches, pasta, stuffed vegetables, and desserts. **Hours: Sunday - Thursday: 9:00 AM - 12:00 AM (midnight), Friday: 9:00 AM - 4:00 PM, Saturday Evening: Until 12:00 AM (midnight). Meals Served: Breakfast, Lunch, & Dinner. Kosher. Reservations preferred. VISA/MasterCard/Diner's. Average Price (Main Course): 21 NIS ($7).**

HaHodit Shel Yermiahu

252 Ben Yehuda Street   **(03) 605-5377**
(corner Yermiyahu Street, near old port of Tel Aviv)

Indian. If you wish to know the restaurant frequented by Zubin Mehta, internationally known conductor of the Israel Philharmonic Orchestra, this is it!! Menu includes six Indian vegetarian dishes such as *Aloo Gobi* -- potatoes with mustard seeds and bay leaves. **Hours: 12:00 PM (noon) - 12:30 AM, Daily. Meals Served: Lunch & Dinner. Smoking Area. Reservations preferred. VISA/MasterCard/Diner's. Foreign Currency accepted. Average Price (Main Course): 18 NIS ($6).**

Hard Rock Cafe

45 Dizengoff Street   **(03) 525-1336**
(at Dizengoff Center)

Mixed. Some organic products used. The famous international rock and roll museum/restaurant is now a fixture of Tel Aviv night life. Menu includes soups, grilled/marinated vegetables, veggie fajita, and veggie burger. **Hours: Sunday - Thursday & Saturday: 11:30 AM - 1:00 AM, Friday: 11:30 AM - 3:00 AM. Meals Served: Lunch & Dinner. Smoking Area. VISA/MasterCard/Diner's/American Express. Traveler's Checks & Foreign Currency accepted. Average Price (Main Course): 30 NIS ($10).**

Hungarian Blintzes

35 Yermiyahu Street   **(03) 605-0674**
(Near old port of Tel Aviv)

Dairy. 18-year-old Hungarian Blintz house. Menu includes soups, blintzes (salty and spicy), sweet blintzes, blintzes with whipped cream. **Hours: Sunday - Thursday: 1:00 PM - 1:00 AM, Friday: Closed, Saturday Evening: Until 1:00 AM. Meals Served: Lunch & Dinner. Kosher. Smoking Area. Reservations preferred. VISA. Foreign Currency accepted. Average Price (Main Course): 18 NIS ($6).**

Indira

Shaul HaMelech 2   (03) 695-4437

Indian. If you do not mind bright green walls and matching green
tablecloths, then Indira might be an option for you. Menu includes
soups, salads, and vegetarian dishes such as *Aloo Dalak* -- spinach with
potatoes or peas. **Hours: Sunday - Thursday: 12:00 PM (noon) - 12:00
AM (midnight), Friday & Saturday: 12:00 PM (noon) - 1:00 AM.
Meals Served: Lunch & Dinner. Reservations preferred. VISA/
MasterCard/Diner's. Average Price (Main Course): 16 NIS ($5.50).**

Judith ✡

Even Gvirol 71 Gan Ha'ir   (03) 527-9214
(City Garden Center Near Municipal Building)

Dairy/Hungarian. Some organic products used. The head manager of
Judith was the principal of the Royal School of Hotel Management in
Budapest and served as the Queen of Belgium's personal baker. A new
Chef is flown in each year from Budapest. Beautiful location, elegant,
and bustling with lots of people. Menu includes soups, salads,
sandwiches, pies, quiche, blintzes, strudel, and cakes. Two speciality
dishes include a vegetarian strudel entrée (with cream) and a vegan
Hungarian dish named *Lecho* -- mixed vegetables with paprika. **Hours:
Sunday - Thursday: 7:30 AM - 1:00 AM, Friday: 7:30 AM - 3:00 PM,
Saturday Evening: Until 1:00 AM. Meals Served: Breakfast, Lunch, &
Dinner. Glatt Kosher. Smoking Area. Reservations preferred.
VISA/MasterCard/Diner's/Eurocard. Foreign Currency accepted.
Average Price (Main Course): 21 NIS ($7).**

Kafe Hafuch

247 Dizengoff Street   (03) 604-2794
(North Dizengoff)

Mixed. 25 - 40 year old crowd. Outdoor/indoor seating. Menu includes
salads, soups, omelettes, sandwiches, blintzes, pasta, quiche, and
desserts. **Hours: Sunday - Thursday: 8:00 AM - 1:00 AM, Friday &
Saturday: 8:00 AM - 4:00 AM. Meals Served: Breakfast, Lunch, &
Dinner. Smoking Area. VISA/MasterCard/Diner's/EuroCard.
Average Price (Main Course): 21 NIS ($7).**

✡ - Recommended Restaurant

Kapulsky

10 Nahalat Binyamin Street   (03) 517-3872
(Pedestrian Mall)

Dairy. On Tuesday and Friday afternoons, artists sell their wares at
stands curving their way through the pedestrian mall and in front of
Kapulsky. Menu includes soups, salads, omelettes, sandwiches, toasts,
pasta, quiche, blintzes, and a large dessert menu. *Kapulsky* serves a
vegetarian schnitzel platter. **Hours: Sunday - Friday: 7:30 AM - 9:00
PM, Saturday: Closed. Meals Served: Breakfast, Lunch, & Dinner.
Smoking Area. VISA/MasterCard/American Express/Diner's. Foreign
Currency accepted. Average Price (Main Course): 22 NIS ($7.50).**

The Library

6 Kaplan Street   (03) 691-6079

Dairy. Situated in the basement of the Hebrew Writer's Association
Building, *The Library* is indeed a library! Pleasant atmosphere. If you
wish to learn about the folk scene in New York, speak to the owner -- he
worked for many years at the Village Gate in Greenwich Village during
the 1960's. Menu includes stuffed potatoes, salads, sandwiches, pasta,
quiche, desserts, and an extensive list of wines and spirits. **Hours:
Sunday - Thursday: 7:30 AM - 12:00 AM (midnight), Friday: 7:30 AM
- 4:00 PM, Saturday: Closed. Meals Served: Breakfast, Lunch, &
Dinner. VISA/MasterCard/Diner's. Average Price (Main Course): 21
NIS ($7).**

Little Old Tel Aviv

300 Hayarkon Street   (03) 605-5539
(near Tel Aviv old port)

Mixed. Large indoor/outdoor seating. Decorated with antique radios
and relics. Menu includes soups, salads, omelettes, pasta, pizza, stuffed
potatoes, desserts, and spirits. **Hours: 12:00 PM (noon) - 2:00 AM,
Daily. Meals Served: Lunch & Dinner. Smoking Area. VISA/
MasterCard/Diner's/American Express. Traveler's Checks & Foreign
Currency accepted. Average Price (Main Course): 18 NIS ($6).**

Paradiso

2 Sprinzak Street   **(03) 695-0383**
(at the Tel Aviv Cinematheque)

Dairy/Italian. Some organic products used. Located in the Cinematheque, Tel Aviv's main center for foreign and classic films. You can see plaques on the walls recognizing the donations of some of America's biggest celebrities to this important cultural institution. Upscale crowd, including actors and the literary set. Menu includes salads, grilled and stir-fried vegetables, foccacia, soups, fettucini (made from whole wheat flour), spaghetti, risotto and pizza, and desserts. **Hours: Sunday - Thursday & Saturday: 12:00 PM (noon) - 1:00 AM, Friday: 12:00 PM (noon) - 3:00 AM. Meals Served: Lunch & Dinner. Reservations preferred. VISA/MasterCard/Diner's. Average Price (Main Course): 20 NIS ($6.50).**

Pinah K'tana

51 Shenkin Street   **(03) 291-850**

Mixed. Friendly, local crowd. The restaurant is very colorful. Indoor/outdoor seating. Menu includes salads, toasts, soups, hummus and techina, vegetable pies, pasta, desserts, and drinks. **Hours: Sunday - Thursday: 8:00 AM - 12:30 AM, Friday: 8:00 AM - 6:00 PM, Saturday: 6:00 PM - 12:30 AM. Meals Served: Breakfast, Lunch, & Dinner. VISA/MasterCard/Diner's/American Express. Average Price (Main Course): 17 NIS ($6).**

Pribar

93 Dizengoff Street   **(03) 522-4501**
(near Frishman)

Juice Bar. Clean, appealing local juice bar offering 25 flavors of fruit shakes plus juices. **Hours: Sunday - Thursday: 9:00 AM - 12:00 AM (midnight), Friday: 9:00 AM - one hour before sundown, Saturday Evening: Until 1:00 AM. No smoking on premises.**

Shangri-La

105 HaYarkon Street   (03) 523-8913
(in the Astor Hotel)

Thai. Some organic products used. Located on the sea front with a view of the Mediterranean. Menu includes soups, Thai traditional salads, noodles, vegetables, and rice. Most dishes served can be prepared vegetarian if a special request is made when ordering. Stir-fried rice noodles with vegetables is a vegan option. **Hours: Sunday - Thursday: 12:30 PM - 12:00 AM (midnight), Friday & Saturday: 12:30 PM - 12:30AM. Meals Served: Lunch & Dinner. Smoking Area. Reservations preferred. VISA/MasterCard/Diner's. Traveler's Checks & Foreign Currency accepted. Average Price (Main Course): 27 NIS ($9).**

Stutz

280 Dizengoff Street   (03) 546-6233
(North Dizengoff)

Mixed. If you want to check out the Israeli singles scene, this is the place. Each table is equipped with a telephone, and if you find someone who catches your fancy, just dial their table number and start up a conversation!! Excellent for improving your Hebrew! Crowd is typically between 20 - 25 years-old. Reservations are a must. Menu includes soups, salads, omelettes, toasts, stuffed potatoes, vegetable pies, pasta, desserts, and 12 different kinds of fruit shakes. **Hours: 9:00 AM - 3:00 AM, Daily. Meals Served: Breakfast, Lunch, & Dinner. Smoking Area. Reservations preferred. VISA/MasterCard/Diner's. Foreign Currency accepted. Average Price (Main Course): 18 NIS ($6).**

Sus Etz (Wooden Horse)

20A Shenkin Street   (03) 528-7955
(opposite Shenkin Park)

Mixed. Some organic products used. A local Shenkin hangout complete with rock music and funky pictures on the walls. Outside seating. Menu includes salads, soups, toasts, sandwiches, pasta, desserts, and spirits menu. **Hours: Sunday - Thursday: 9:00 AM - 1:00 AM, Friday: 8:00 AM - 6:00 PM, Saturday: 5:30 PM - 1:00 AM.. Meals Served: Breakfast, Lunch & Dinner. VISA/MasterCard/Diner's. Average Price (Main Course): 20 NIS ($6.50).**

Tandoori ✡

2 Zamenhoff Street   **(03) 296-185/296-605**
(Dizengoff Square)

Indian. A top class dining experience of superb Indian food. Reena
Pushkarna, is this restaurant's owner and you are likely to find her
visiting each table asking how you have enjoyed your meal or offering a
scented flower as a small reminder of your visit there. Menu includes a
vegetarian section featuring dishes such as *saag paneer* (spinach puree),
aloo dum (potatoes cooked with tomatoes and hyderabi spices), and
sabzi jalfrezi (mixed vegetables flavored with herbs and spices served in
curry sauce). They will prepare a full vegan meal on request, and their
clientele includes Indian Jains who trade on the Ramat Gan Diamond
Exchange. **Hours: Sunday - Friday: 12:30 AM - 3:30 PM and 7:00 PM -
1:00 AM, Saturday: 1:00 PM - 4:00 PM (lunch buffet) and 7:00 PM -
1:00 AM. Meals Served: Lunch & Dinner. Reservations required.
VISA/MasterCard/American Express/Diner's. Foreign Currency &
Traveler's Checks accepted. Average Price (Main Course): 18 NIS
($6).**

Tatoo

185 Ben Yehuda Street   **(03) 546-8808**

Dairy. Menu includes salads, vegetable pies, sandwiches, toasts, and
desserts. **Hours: 10:00 AM - 1:00 AM, Daily. Meals Served:
Breakfast, Lunch, & Dinner. Smoking Area. VISA/MasterCard/
Diner's/American Express. Foreign Currency accepted. Average
Price (Main Course): 20 NIS ($6.50).**

Ten Li Chow

3 Yordei Hasira Street   **(03) 665-956/617-755**
(near Old Port of Tel Aviv)

Chinese. Menu includes vegetarian dishes such as eggplant in hot garlic
sauce, mixed vegetables, and mushroom and bamboo shoots. **Hours:
Sunday - Thursday: 12:30 PM - 11:30 PM, Friday: Closed, Saturday
Evening: Until 12:00 AM (midnight). Meals Served: Lunch & Dinner.
Glatt Kosher. Smoking Area. Reservations preferred. VISA/
MasterCard/American Express/Diner's. Traveler's Checks & Foreign
Currency accepted. Average Price (Main Course): 25 NIS ($8.50).**

✡ **- Recommended Restaurant**

Tivoli

98 Dizengoff Street   (03) 524-9797
(near Frishman)

Mixed. Menu includes soups, salads, toasts, omelettes, baked potatoes, pizza, pasta, blintzes, pancakes, and desserts. **Hours: 8:30 AM - 12:30 AM, Daily. Meals Served: Breakfast, Lunch, & Dinner. Smoking Area. VISA/MasterCard/Diner's/American Express/EuroCard. Average Price (Main Course): 21 NIS ($7).**

Tnuva at the Opera

1 Allenby Street   (03) 517-1847
(in the Opera Tower)

Dairy. Located in one of Tel Aviv's newest and most beautiful buildings -- the Opera House -- which combines exclusive shopping, luxury apartments and restaurants under one roof. *Tnuva* has both indoor seating and an outside veranda overlooking the Mediterranean. Menu includes soups, salads, omelettes, toasts, vegetable pies, blintzes, vegetarian schnitzel and burger platters, pasta, stuffed potatoes, and desserts. **Hours: Sunday - Thursday: 8:00 AM - 2:00 AM, Friday & Saturday: 8:00 AM - 4:00 AM. Meals Served: Breakfast, Lunch, & Dinner. Smoking Area. Reservations preferred. VISA/MasterCard/ Diner's/American Express. Foreign Currency accepted. Average Price (Main Course): 20 NIS ($6.50).**

Tnuva Shelanu

41 Frishman Street   (03) 522-0297
(corner of Dizengoff Street)

Dairy. Menu includes appetizers, soups, salads, toasts, croissants, quiche, blintzes, pasta, omelettes, and hot Chinese spaghetti with vegetables, walnuts, and soy sauce. **Hours: Sunday - Friday: 8:00 AM - 1:00 AM, Saturday: 9:00 AM - 2:30 AM. Meals Served: Breakfast, Lunch, & Dinner. Smoking Area. VISA/MasterCard/Diner's. Traveler's Checks & Foreign Currency accepted. Average Price (Main Course): 18 NIS ($6).**

Tnuvaleh

Dizengoff Center (Gate #3)   **(03) 204-369**

Dairy. Menu includes soups, salads, pasta, stuffed potatoes, sandwiches, omelettes, quiche, blintzes, and desserts. **Hours: Sunday - Thursday: 9:30 AM - 10:30 PM, Friday: 9:30 AM - 3:00 PM, Saturday Evening: Until 11:30 PM. Meals Served: Breakfast, Lunch, & Dinner. Kosher. VISA/MasterCard/Diner's. Average Price (Main Course): 18 NIS ($6).**

Yotvata in Town ✿

Herbert Samuel Promenade   **(03) 510-4667**
(Tel Aviv Beach Front)

Dairy. Part of *Kibbutz Yotvata Restaurant Chain.* Lots of seating, but it is quite popular, so best to make reservations. Upstairs seating with view of the sea. Menu includes toast melts, salads, cheese platters, soups, pizza, pancakes, and stuffed potatoes. The natural fruit juices are not to be missed!! Large portions. **Hours: 7:00 AM - 4:00 AM, Daily. Moderately Priced.**

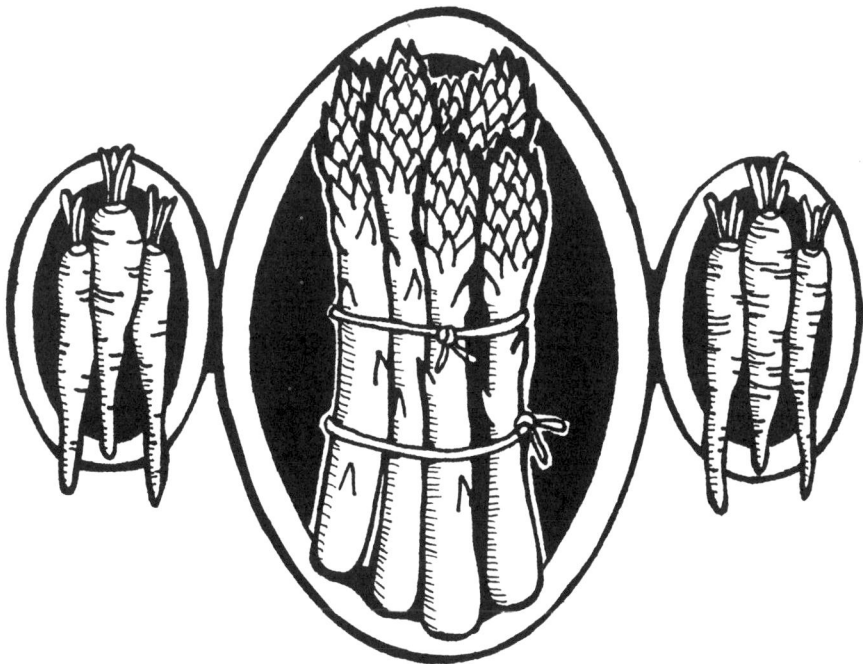

✿ **Recommended Restaurant**

Jaffa

Jaffa is officially part of Tel Aviv, but it is a distinct location. Jaffa is a delightful place to visit if you are interested in archaeology, enjoy visiting artists' studios, and love the smell of the fresh ocean air. Being a fishing wharf, Jaffa has an over-abundance of fish restaurants which leaves very few options for vegetarians. These were a few places that I was able to excavate:

Aladin

5 Mifratz Shlomo Street   **(03) 682-6766**
(at approach to the old city)

Mixed. Located in a building which has a rich history as both a Turkish bathhouse and brothel 600 years ago. Splendid view of the sea. Indoor/outdoor seating. Menu includes soups, Mediterranean salads, vegetable pies, blintzes, and desserts. **Hours: 12:00 PM (noon) - 1:00 AM, Daily. Meals Served: Lunch & Dinner. VISA/MasterCard/ Diner's/American Express. Foreign Currency accepted. Average Price (Main Course): 18 NIS ($6).**

Night Toast

26 Raziel Street   **(03) 681-7947**
(main street in the new city of Jaffa)

Dairy. Make your own toast by choosing from various vegetable stuffings. Also serves salads. **Hours: 9:00 AM - 5:00 PM, Daily. Meals Served: Breakfast & Lunch. Average Price (Main Course): 6 NIS ($2).**

Taj Mahal

12 Kikar Kedumim (old city)   **(03) 682-1002**

Indian. **Hours: 12:00 PM (noon) - 3:00 PM and 7:00 PM - 12:00 AM (midnight), Daily.**

Thai Loti

28 Raziel Street   **(03) 683-2670**
(main street in the new city of Jaffa)

Fruits/Desserts. Started by an Israeli who lived one and half years in
Thailand and became enamored with this Thai dessert. The *Thailoti* is a
pancake fried on a wok stuffed with fruits and toppings of your choice.
Hours: 10:00 AM - 2:00 AM, Daily.

Haifa

Haifa sits on the Carmel Mountain, overlooking the Mediterranean and the port which has made it a major commercial and shipping center in Israel. A beautiful city, with a working yet "laid back" atmosphere. The co-existence between Arab and Jewish residents of the city can be seen in work and play. Getting around is easy; either by bus or the *Carmelite* -- a one line subway that goes up and down Mount Carmel and stops at all important tourist destinations. Geographically, Haifa is fairly simple. There are three major areas, which contain all the restaurants in this listing:

Hadar -- An older area, with lots of small shops and falafel stands. The two main streets are Herzl Boulevard and HaNevi'im. The Nordau Pedestrian Mall (parallel to Herzl Blvd.) is where most restaurants are concentrated.

Central Carmel -- The "upscale" part of Haifa, with a spectacular view of the city and port. The main street is HaNassi, which ends at the Panorama Center, a small mall adjacent to the Dan Panorama Hotel. The other end of HaNassi becomes Moriyya Boulevard, which eventually leads to the Haifa University and Technion.

Downtown Area -- Influenced by the Haifa Port, this is the business center of Haifa, which thrives during the day but closes up after 5:00 PM.

Alain ✡

Ha'atzmaut Street 149　　　　　　　　　　　**(04) 664-891**
(Downtown area)

Dairy. A coffee house with a lunch buffet. Legal and business crowd. Manager is very accommodating. Menu includes lunch buffet with a variety of vegetarian choices such as cooked vegetables, pies, and salads. **Hours: Sunday - Friday: 7:00 AM - 4:00 PM, Saturday: Closed. Meals Served: Breakfast & Lunch. Kosher. VISA/MasterCard/Diner's/ American Express. Foreign Currency accepted. Average Price (Main Course): 21 NIS ($7).**

Alexandra

Haim Street 2　　　　　　　　　　　**(04) 625-505**

Mixed. Menu includes soups, salads, toasts, omelettes, vegetable pies, spaghetti, pizza, crepes, and pancakes. **Hours: Sunday - Thursday: 8:00 AM - 12:00 AM (midnight), Friday: 8:00 AM - 3:00 AM, Saturday: 4:00 PM - 1:00 AM. Meals Served: Breakfast, Lunch, Dinner. Smoking Area. VISA/MasterCard/Diner's/American Express. Foreign Currency accepted. Average Price (Main Course): 17.50 NIS ($5.50).**

Aquarelle

33 Moriya Street　　　　　　　　　　　**(04) 373-454**
(A bit outside of Central Carmel area)

Mixed. Nice atmosphere. Older, yuppie crowd, 30+. Indoor/outdoor seating. Menu includes salads and cheese dishes. **Hours: Sunday - Thursday: 5:30 PM - 1:00 AM, Friday: 5:00 PM - 2:30 AM, Saturday: 6:30 PM - 2:30 AM. Meals Served: Dinner only. Average Price: 21 NIS ($7).**

✡ Recommended Restaurant

The Bank

119 Hanassi Street   (04) 389-623
(Central Carmel)

Mixed. A very "in" coffee house frequented by people of all ages. Always a crowd, especially in the evenings. Menu includes soup, salads, toasts, blintzes, cheese platters, baked potatoes, pancakes, and desserts. **Hours: Sunday - Thursday: 8:00 AM - 1:30 AM, Friday & Saturday: 8:00 AM - 2:30 AM. Meals Served: Breakfast, Lunch, & Dinner. VISA/Master-Card/Diner's/American Express. Foreign Currency accepted. Average Price (Main Course): NIS 18 ($6).**

Bursa

119 Hanassi Street   (04) 381-487
(Central Carmel)

Dairy. Very "in" place, 25+ crowd. Indoor/outdoor seating. Menu includes soups, salads, sandwiches, toasts, blintzes, pancakes, and desserts. **Hours: Sunday - Thursday: 8:00 AM - 2:00 AM, Friday & Saturday: 8:00 AM - 3:00 AM. Meals Served: Breakfast, Lunch, & Dinner. VISA/MasterCard/Diner's/American Express. Foreign Currency accepted. Average Price (Main Course): 17 NIS ($5.50).**

California

1 Haim Street   (04) 672-628
(Hadar- Nordau Pedestrian Mall)

Mixed. Younger crowd, 25-35 years-old. Live music on Friday. Lots of indoor/outdoor seating. Menu includes salads, baked potatoes, sand-wiches, spaghetti, and a vegan dish - couscous with cooked vegetables. **Hours: Sunday - Thursday: 9:00 AM - 1:00 AM, Friday: 8:30 AM - 4:00 PM and 10:00 PM - 3:00 AM, Saturday: 5:00 PM - 3:00 AM. Meals Served: Breakfast, Lunch, & Dinner. VISA/MasterCard/Diner's/American Express. Average Price (Main Course): 12 NIS ($4).**

Chaim Vegetarian Restaurant ✡

30 Herzl Street (Hadar)   (04) 674-667

Dairy. Be forewarned that *Chaim Vegetarian* does serve fish!! This 60-year-old establishment has the feel of a Jewish Restaurant on the Lower East Side of New York. Hope you enjoy the yellow tables!! Menu includes soups, salads, pancakes, blintzes, noodle pies, cooked vegetables, stuffed cabbage, and juices. **Hours: Sunday - Thursday: 9:00 AM - 7:00 PM, Friday: 9:00 AM - 2:00 PM, Saturday: Closed. Meals Served: Lunch & Dinner. Average Price (Main Course): 18 NIS ($6).**

Croque

60 Moriyya Street   (04) 242-668
(Central Carmel)

Mixed. French atmosphere, 20-40 year old crowd. Menu includes soups, salads, bagels, and toasts. **Hours: Sunday - Thursday & Saturday: 7:00 PM - 12:30 AM, Friday: 8:00 PM - 1:30 AM. VISA/MasterCard. Average Price (Main Course): 21 NIS ($7).**

Kapulsky

111 Hanassi Street   (04) 373-029
(Central Carmel)

Dairy. Menu includes soups, salads, omelettes, sandwiches, toasts, pasta, quiche, blintzes, and a large dessert menu. **Hours: Sunday - Thursday: 8:00 AM - 1:00 AM, Friday & Saturday: 8:00 AM - 2:00 AM. Meals Served: Breakfast, Lunch & Dinner. VISA/MasterCard/Diner's. Traveler's Checks & Foreign Currency accepted. Average Price (Main Course): 24 NIS ($8).**

Prego

20 Nordau Street   (04) 623-520
(Hadar- Nordau Pedestrian Mall)

Italian. Elegant, upscale crowd. Menu includes pasta and pizza. **Hours: 12:00 PM (noon) - 12:00 AM (midnight), Daily. Meals Served: Lunch & Dinner. VISA/MasterCard/Diner's/American Express.**

✡ Recommended Restaurant

Rothschild's

140 Hanassi Street   (04) 360-070/1
(Central Carmel, next to Haifa Cultural Center)

Mixed. Upscale atmosphere. Indoor/outdoor seating. Menu includes soups, salads, vegetable pies, stuffed vegetables, pasta, and desserts. Serves afternoon coffee and cake between 4:00 PM - 6:00 PM. **Hours: Sunday - Thursday: 9:00 AM - 1:00 AM, Friday: 9:00 AM - 3:00 AM, Saturday: 10:00 AM - 1:30 AM. Meals Served: Breakfast, Lunch, & Dinner. VISA/MasterCard/Diner's/American Express. Foreign Currency accepted. Average Price (Main Course): NIS 21 ($7).**

Viennese Gallery ✡

107 Hanassi Street   (04) 352-222
(Central Carmel, at the Dan Panorama Hotel)

Dairy. Gorgeous place to have a break from the hustle and bustle of the city. The *Gallery* is true Vienna, complete with pastries and elderly gentlemen in ties and jackets - who may have immigrated from Vienna many years ago! Wonderful view of Haifa Port. Menu includes soups, salads, blintzes, pasta, sandwiches, omelettes, and desserts. **Hours: Sunday - Thursday: 10:00 AM - 11:30 PM, Friday & Saturday: 10:00 AM - 1:00 AM. Meals Served: Lunch & Dinner. Kosher (Hotel certificate). Smoking Area. VISA/MasterCard/Diner's/American Express. Traveler's Checks & Foreign Currency accepted. Average Price (Main Course): NIS 33 ($11).**

The White Gallery

125 Hanassi Street (Central Carmel)   (04) 375-574

Mixed. Newly opened restaurant and art gallery, with exhibits of different Israeli artists throughout the year. Yuppie crowd, classy atmosphere, and wood floors. Menu includes soups, salads, bagel toasts, pasta, and desserts. **Hours: Sunday - Thursday: 8:00 AM - 1:00 AM, Friday: 8:00 AM - 4:00 AM, Saturday: 8:00 AM - 2:00 AM. Meals Served: Breakfast, Lunch, & Dinner. VISA/MasterCard/Diner's/American Express. Foreign Currency accepted. Average Price (Main Course): NIS 24 ($8).**

✡ Recommended Restaurant

Tiberias

Tiberias, located on the Sea of Galilee, is a small town with a big lake and is a wonderful springboard for trips to Northern Israel. Since the days of Jesus of Nazareth, Tiberias has been known for fishing, and, unfortunately this has made for a proliferation of fish restaurants in the modern day city. I did manage to locate some places for the vegetarian to eat. Tiberias is divided into the following areas:

The Pedestrian Mall (Tayelet) -- Between Habanim Street and the Lake, there are a number of restaurants here.

Habanim Street -- Main road where major hotels are located, plus a few falafel/Middle Eastern restaurants.

The Lake Promenade -- The general lake area.

The Marina -- An indoor "mini-mall" on The Wharf (still under construction) that contains restaurants. There might be other eating options after the Marina is completed.

Cherry
Tiberias Pedestrian Mall   **(06) 790-051**

Dairy. Menu includes soups, salads, omelettes, toasts, vegetable pie, blintzes, stuffed vegetables, pasta, desserts, and juices. **Hours: Sunday - Thursday, Friday: 8:00 AM - 3:00 AM, Saturday: 7:30 AM - 3:00 AM. Meals Served: Breakfast, Lunch, & Dinner. VISA/MasterCard/ American Express. Foreign Currency accepted. Average Price (Main Course): 21 NIS ($7).**

Hard Rock Restaurant

The Marina (on the lake side)   (06) 722-681

Mixed. Not the famous *Hard Rock Cafe*, but a nice try anyhow!! Seating on the lake. Becomes a crowded pub at night. Menu includes soups, salads, Mediterranean salads, toasts, omelettes, pasta, pizza, and desserts. **Hours: Sunday - Thursday: 8:00 AM - 12:00 AM (midnight), Friday & Saturday: 8:00 AM - 1:00 AM. Meals Served: Breakfast, Lunch, & Dinner. Reservations Preferred. VISA/MasterCard/Diner's. Traveler's Checks & Foreign Currency accepted. Average Price (Main Course): 21 NIS ($7).**

Kapulsky

Pedestrian Mall   (06) 720-341

Dairy. Menu includes soups, salads, omelettes, sandwiches, toasts, pasta, blintzes, and a large selection of desserts. **Hours: 8:00 AM - 2:00 AM, Daily. Meals Served: Breakfast, Lunch, & Dinner. Smoking Area. VISA/MasterCard/Diner's. Traveler's Checks & Foreign Currency accepted. Average Price (Main Course): 21 NIS ($7).**

Karamba Restaurant ✿

Lake Promenade   (06) 791-546/724-505

Dairy. Tropical atmosphere. Sit under a thatched hut roof and sip fruit drinks while listening to lively music. Young crowd at night with lots of dancing. Menu includes soups, salads, quiche, vegetable crepes and pies, pizza, stuffed potatoes, whole wheat bread, fruits, and desserts. **Hours: 10:00 AM - 2:00 AM, Daily. Meals Served: Lunch & Dinner. Reservations preferred. VISA/MasterCard/American Express/Diner's. Traveler's Checks & Foreign Currency accepted. Average Price (Main Course): 23 NIS ($7.50).**

Kohinoor

Moriah Plaza Hotel (Lake Promenade)   (06) 724-939

Indian. This is the "kosher version" of the *Tandoori Indian Restaurant*, with kosher certification. **For full description, see listing for *Tandoori* in Tel Aviv.**

✿ Recommended Restaurant

Mama Mia

Pedestrian Mall (06) 792-484

Dairy. Nice atmosphere. Clean. Indoor/outdoor seating. Menu includes soups, salads, toasts, omelettes, stuffed potatoes, pasta, pizza, *melawach* (Yemenite fried dough), blintzes, and desserts. **Hours: Sunday - Thursday: 9:30 AM - 12:30 AM, Friday: 9:30 AM - one hour before sundown, Saturday Evening: Until 1:00 AM. Meals Served: Breakfast, Lunch, & Dinner. Kosher. VISA/MasterCard/Diner's/ American Express. Traveler's Checks & Foreign Currency accepted. Average Price (Main Course): 18 NIS ($6).**

Marina Sunrise

Marina (on the lake side) (06) 723-303

Dairy. Seating on the lake. Lively pub at night. Menu includes soups, salads, *melawach* (Yemenite fried dough), baked potatoes, omelettes, pasta, pizza, blintzes, and desserts. **Hours: Sunday - Thursday: 8:30 AM - 12:00 AM (midnight), Friday & Saturday: 8:30 AM - 3:00 AM. Meals Served: Breakfast, Lunch, & Dinner. VISA/MasterCard/Diner's/ American Express. Traveler's Checks & Foreign Currency accepted. Average Price (Main Course): 15 NIS ($5).**

The Galilee:
Resorts and Restaurants

The Galilee region, with its rolling green hills and fertile plains is an ideal area to enjoy nature's beauty and eat wholesome food. To our good fortune, there are some wonderful resorts and restaurants in the Galilee area. It is highly recommended to plan a 2-3 day trip and take advantage of at least one of these wonderful vacation sites and try to visit the others. Some careful planning, a car, and a bit of a travel budget will make this excursion that much more enjoyable.

Hotel Mizpe Hayamim ✡

Rosh Pina   **(06) 937-014/937-013**
(On Rosh Pina-Safed Road)

Dairy. Some organic products used. Set in 30 acres of natural forest in the hills above Rosh Pina in Northern Galilee, Mizpe Hayamim is a well-known resort for vegetarians and those seeking a quiet time in nature. From the hotel are beautiful views of the Sea of Galilee, Hula Nature Reserve, and Golan Heights. The hotel, recently opened after extensive renovation and enlargement, has been furnished in a rustic European style, accented with flowers and antique ornamentation. A busy hotel that is frequented by both overseas groups and Israelis, you should reserve well in advance, preferably before leaving for Israel. To give one an idea of price, a full board double room for one night ranges from $115 on weekdays to $142 on weekends -- note that prices change during the season. Facilities include swimming pools, jacuzzi, steam room and dry sauna, herbal mineral baths, massage, Shiatsu, Yoga and Tai-Chi classes, plus hikes and evening entertainment. The food served is vegetarian, (although they serve fish) and their vegetables, cheese, and olive oil are produced on the premises without the use of pesticides or artificial preservatives. **Restaurant Hours: 8:00 AM - 10:00 AM, 1:00 PM - 3:00 PM, and 7:00 PM - 9:00 PM. Meals Served: Breakfast, Lunch, Dinner. No Smoking on Premises. Reservations necessary. VISA/ MasterCard/American Express. Traveler's Checks & Foreign Currency accepted. Average Meal Price: 60 NIS ($20).**

✿ Recommended Restaurant

Maharishi Ayur-Veda Health Center

Hararit   (06) 781-575
(near Carmiel)

Vegetarian. A health center that stresses preventative medicine and techniques, under the supervision of a licensed Israeli medical doctor. Natural treatments to relieve stress and cure respiratory problems. Herbal steam baths. Call for costs of treatments and lodging. Meals are vegetarian without eggs (check to see if they use milk products). **Hours: 9:00 AM - 2:30 PM, Daily. Meals Served: Lunch. No Smoking on Premises. Reservations preferred. VISA/MasterCard/ EuroCard. Traveler's Checks & Foreign Currency accepted. Average Meal Price: 25 NIS ($8.50).**

Taiko Japanese Tea House ✿

Mitzpe Michmanim   (04) 884-989
(near Carmiel)

Japanese. Some organic products used. A traditional Japanese Tea House located in a small community near Carmiel. The restaurant is located in the home of Taiko, a Japanese woman who creates original Kimonos. From the house, located in the hills, one can see all of the lower Galilee including the Golan Heights. Call first to arrange a meal, and you can discuss the menu with Taiko. Menu includes miso soup, seaweed plate, tempura, and main dishes. **Hours: By appointment only. Meals Served: Lunch & Dinner. No Smoking on Premises. VISA/MasterCard. Traveler's Checks & Foreign Currency accepted. Complete Meal Price: 68 NIS ($22.50).**

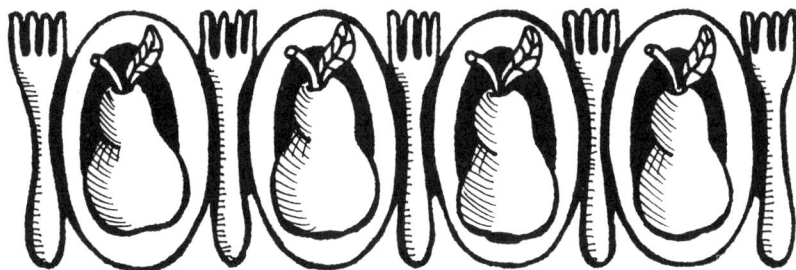

✿ Recommended Restaurant

Moshav Amirim ✡

Amirim, whose name literally means *tree tops* is located on the road to Safed. It claims to be the "only Vegetarian-Naturist village in the world." The word "naturist" in Hebrew also translates to "vegan," so this really is a paradise for the vegetarian traveler. Established in 1958, *Amirim* sits 800 meters above the Sea of Galilee, affording a spectacular view. Staying at *Amirim* will also give one the flavor of life on an Israeli *moshav* -- a collective settlement where land is jointly owned, but homes are individual property. A stay at *Amirim* is a vegetarian's dream, both in the gastronomic sense and having a common bond with your hosts. I was informed by one of the guest-house owners that most visitors to *Amirim* are not vegetarians, but are quite impressed with the food and tranquility of the area.

Many homes at *Amirim* are either restaurants and/or guest houses, serving vegetarian and vegan meals. Other facilities available include a swimming pool, tea house, movies, lectures, tours, a synagogue, and alternative medicine treatments. Prices for meals are about 50 NIS ($16.50) at most homes, and lodging prices should be checked individually. **Hours listed below can vary according to season, so it is important to make telephone reservations for meals. The general number at *Amirim* is (06) 989-571 or 989-203. The following is a listing of some of the homes that I visited:**

Carmeli Restaurant
Moshav Amirim   **(06) 989-316**

Vegetarian. Many organic products used. Aviva Carmeli, the proprietor, is a wonderful person who knows many members of the Jewish Vegetarian Society. Inside and patio seating. She has rooms for rent. Menu includes soups, salads, grains, soy dishes, pies, cooked vegetables, fruit, cake, and herbal teas. Serves organic vegetables, organic cheese, and free range eggs. **Hours: 9:00 AM - 9:00 PM, Daily. Meals Served: Breakfast, Lunch, and Dinner. No Smoking on premises. Reservations preferred. Traveler's Checks & Foreign Currency accepted. Average Meal Price: NIS 50 ($16.50).**

✡ **Recommended**

Dalia's Restaurant
Moshav Amirim   (06) 989-349

Vegetarian. Some organic products used. Dine in Dalia's private garden
with a view of Kinneret. Menu includes soups, salads, stuffed vegetables,
blintzes, and almond croquettes. **Hours: 8:00 AM - 8:00 PM, Daily.
Meals Served: Breakfast, Lunch, & Dinner. Kosher. No Smoking on
premises. VISA/MasterCard. Traveler's Checks & Foreign Currency
accepted. Average Meal Price: 36 NIS ($12).**

Hamiel Restaurant
Moshav Amirim   (06) 989-746

Vegetarian/Middle Eastern. Some organic products used. Has a
beautiful new guest house, which has two bedrooms and a loft for
couples or large families. Menu includes soups, Mediterranean salads,
stuffed vegetables, moussaka, vegetable pies, and desserts. **Hours: 8:30
AM - 8:30 PM, Daily. Meals Served: Breakfast, Lunch, & Dinner. No
Smoking on premises. Foreign Currency accepted. Average Meal
Price: 50 NIS ($16.50).**

HaSeudah HaAhronah (The Last Supper)
Moshav Amirim   (06) 989-788

Vegetarian/Balkan. Some organic products used. The restaurant is also
decorated with antique furniture, wooden floors, and a beautiful garden.
View the many works of art displayed while listening to classical music.
Menu includes baked bread with garden spices, natural drinks, ten types
of salads, variety of cooked vegetables, moussaka, stuffed mushrooms,
and almond cutlets. Desserts include seasonal fruit, herbal tea, nut
cakes, and honey. **Hours: 1:30 PM - 9:00 PM, Daily. Meals Served:
Lunch & Dinner. No Smoking on Premises. Reservations Preferred.
Foreign Currency accepted. Meal Price: 70 NIS ($23).**

Nitai
Moshav Amirim   **(06) 980-816**

Vegetarian/Indian. Some organic products used. Primarily take-out food for a "box lunch" on a trip in the Galilee. I was informed that Theodore Nitai, the owner, may be relocating to Jerusalem to learn Indian philosophy and Sanskrit, so call before you come. Menu includes salads, vegetarian Indian menu, and fruit juices. **Hours: By appointment. Meals Served: Lunch & Dinner. No Smoking on premises. Average Meal Price: 36 NIS ($12).**

Eilat

Eilat, the southernmost point of the country, is Israel's capital of fun and sun. With a European atmosphere, Eilat is a city that has much to offer in the way of night life, coral reefs, desert trips, and a point from which to travel to both Egypt and Jordan (it is still hard to believe I am writing this!). Most restaurants in Eilat are found on the Seaside Promenade on the Northern Beach, along the rest of the waterfront, or at the edge of the city of Eilat which faces the beach area. And remember, the dry desert temperatures range to over 100 degrees during the summer, with low humidity. It is important to keep drinking liquids all day to avoid dehydration and a tired feeling.

Apropro

Philip Murray House   **(07) 374-337**
(City of Eilat, Hatmarim Street)

Dairy. Situated in the cultural building of Eilat. Musical performances on weekends. Menu includes salads, omelettes, sandwiches and toasts, pasta, crepes, desserts, and a spirit menu. There is a special Thai menu consisting of vegetable and noodle dishes. **Hours: Sunday - Thursday: 8:00 AM - 2:00 AM, Friday & Saturday: 5:00 PM - 2:00 AM. Meals Served: Breakfast, Lunch, & Dinner. Smoking Area. VISA/ MasterCard/Diner's. Traveler's Checks & Foreign Currency accepted. Average Price (Main Course): 21 NIS ($7).**

Cafe Royal

King Solomon Hotel   **(07) 334-111**
(Northern Beach Promenade)

Dairy. Nice atmosphere, entrances both on promenade and from hotel. Young, upscale crowd. Classical music in the evenings. Indoor/outdoor seating. Menu includes soups, salads, pasta, vegetable pies, baked potatoes, and blintzes. **Hours: Sunday - Thursday: 12:30 PM - 3:00 PM and 6:00 PM - 12:00 AM (midnight), Friday & Saturday: 12:30 PM - 3:00 PM and 7:00 PM - 12:00 AM (midnight). Meals Served: Breakfast, Lunch, & Dinner. Smoking Area. VISA/MasterCard/ Diner's/American Express. Traveler's Checks & Foreign Currency accepted. Average Price (Main Course): 24 NIS ($8).**

A Good Harvest

Pearl Center   **(07) 374-723**
(Northern Beach Promenade)

Dairy. Simple atmosphere, large selection of vegetarian dishes. Menu includes salads (16 types), stuffed potatoes, pasta, blintzes, cooked vegetables, pancakes, soy burgers, and natural juices. **Hours: 9:00 AM - 1:00 AM, Daily. Meals Served: Breakfast, Lunch, & Dinner. VISA/ MasterCard/Diner's. Foreign Currency accepted. Average Price (Main Course): 15 NIS ($5).**

Kapulsky

Pearl Center (Northern Beach Promenade)   **(07) 376-510**

Dairy. Popular cafe, favorite tourist spot. Indoor/outdoor seating. Menu includes soups, salads, omelettes, sandwiches, toasts, pasta, quiche, blintzes, and a large dessert selection. **Hours: 9:00 AM - 12:00 AM (midnight), Daily. Meals Served: Breakfast, Lunch, & Dinner. Smoking Area. VISA/MasterCard/American Express/Diner's. Foreign Currency accepted. Average Price (Main Course): 18 NIS ($6).**

La Festivale

Shalom Center   **(07) 374-922**
(City of Eilat, Hatamarim Street)

Dairy. Large outdoor seating, central location. Menu includes salads, baguettes, toasts, omelettes, pasta, pizza, falafel, vegetable pies, baked potatoes, blintzes, pancakes, and fruit shakes. **Hours: 7:00 AM - 1:00 AM, Daily. Meals Served: Breakfast, Lunch, & Dinner. Reservations preferred. VISA/MasterCard/Diner's. Foreign Currency accepted. Average Price (Main Course): 15 NIS ($5).**

La Terrace

Moriah Plaza Hotel   **(07) 361-111**
(Northern Beach Promenade)

Dairy. Exquisite poolside atmosphere, with indoor seating. Dancing and live singing in summer. Menu includes salads, toasts, sandwiches, quiche, and desserts. **Hours: 10:00 AM - 11:00 PM, Daily. Meals Served: Lunch & Dinner. Kosher (hotel certificate). Smoking Area. VISA/MasterCard/Diner's/American Express. Traveler's Checks & Foreign Currency accepted. Average Price (Main Course): 24 NIS ($8).**

Tandoori

King's Wharf   **(07) 333-666**
(Northern Beach Promenade beneath the Lagoona Hotel)

Indian. **For full description, see listing for *Tandoori* Tel Aviv.**

Trattoria

Moriah Plaza Hotel   **(07) 361-111**
(Northern Beach Promenade)

Italian/Dairy. Elegant atmosphere. Menu includes vegetable hor d'oeuvres, soups, pizza, pasta, and desserts. **Hours: 7:00 PM - 11:00 PM, Daily. Kosher (hotel certificate). Smoking Area. Reservations preferred. VISA/MasterCard/Diner's/American Express. Traveler's Checks & Foreign Currency accepted. Average Price (Main Course): 30 NIS ($10).**

Health Food Stores In Israel

Jerusalem

Adamah
45 Ussishkin Street

Sells organic vegetables and foods.

(02) 259-823

American - Israeli Natural Foods
76 Jaffa Road

Distributor of Sunrider products in Israel.

(02) 384-069

Duvduvan
99 Agrippas Street (Mahane Yehuda Market)

(02) 234-859

Happy Life
2 Yeshiahu Street

(02) 373-497

Health Food Store
Malcha Jerusalem Mall (Ground floor), Jerusalem

(02) 784-693

Ma'dani HaTeva
29 Gaza Street, Jerusalem

Sells organic vegetables.

(02) 632-270

Mercaz HaBriut
59 HaPisga Street (Bayit Vagan)

(02) 420-750

The Natural Way
Denia Square (Beit Hakerem shopping center)

Sells organic vegetables. Free deliveries for tourists.

(02) 523-644

Naturalis
17 Yoel Solomon Street (Nahalat Shiva)

(02) 246-376

Teva Shani
31 Beit Lechem Way

Sells organic vegetables.

(02) 732-323

Tel Aviv

Beit Teva Shai
16 Masryk Square   (03) 524-1172
   Sells organic vegetables.

Beit Teva Tsafen
58 Yehudah Maccabi Street (North Tel Aviv)   (03) 544-4292

Beit Teva V'Hadieta
217 Allenby Street (in the passageway)   (03) 295-783

Dikla
45 King George Street   (03) 528-4841
   Sells organic vegetables.

Dr. Teva
133 Ibn Gvriol Street, Tel Aviv   (03) 546-0850

Ha'ikar Ha'Briut
47 Ibn Gvriol Street   (03) 691-8506

Ha'ikar Habriut
18 Ashtori Hafrachi Street (near Bazel St., North Tel Aviv)   (03) 544-4432
   Sells organic vegetables.

Har Duf
2 Levontin Street   (03) 560-0596
   Sells organic vegetables.

Manah Teva
10 Hadar Yosef Street   (03) 647-8480
   Sells organic vegetables.

Naturalis
Dizengoff Center (2nd Floor)   (03) 528-0170

Paz
14A Shenkin Street   (03) 528-2075

Zanbar
6 HaSharon Street (at the old central bus station)   (03) 370-419
   Sells organic vegetables.

Greater Tel Aviv Area

Bnei Brak: Dr. Teva
44 Rabbi Akiva Street

(03) 579-5406

Givatayim: Natural Choice
33 Weizman Street

(03) 320-201

Holon: Te'evonit Neot Shoshanim
44 Geulim Street

(03) 559-6432

Petach Tikva: Beit HaBriut V'Hateva
27 Moliver Street

(03) 930-6812

Ra'anna: Bio-Center
Moshav Givat Chen

(03) 982-317

> Farming settlement near Ra'anna that sells their own organic vegetables and foods.

Ramat Aviv: Teva Farm
30 Tagor Street

(03) 642-1458

> Sells organic vegetables.

Ramat HaSharon: TevaLand
16 Ushishkin Street

(03) 549-5170

Rishon LeZion: Beit Teva Yuval
48 Jabotinsky Street
(inside Gindi passage), Rishon LeZion

(03) 967-3694

> Sells organic vegetables.

Tevi Li
4 HaHistadrut Street

(03) 930-8460

> Sells organic vegetables.

Haifa

Cannan Hadar
7 Herzl Street

(04)627-505

Dieteti - Col
24 Jaffa Street

(04) 678-176/666-997

Ha'Trufa Ha'Tivit
57 Herzl Street

(04) 640-611

Labriut
124 Hanassi Boulevard (Central Carmel)

(04) 388-392

Teva Farm
30 Jaffa Street, Haifa,

(04)666-640

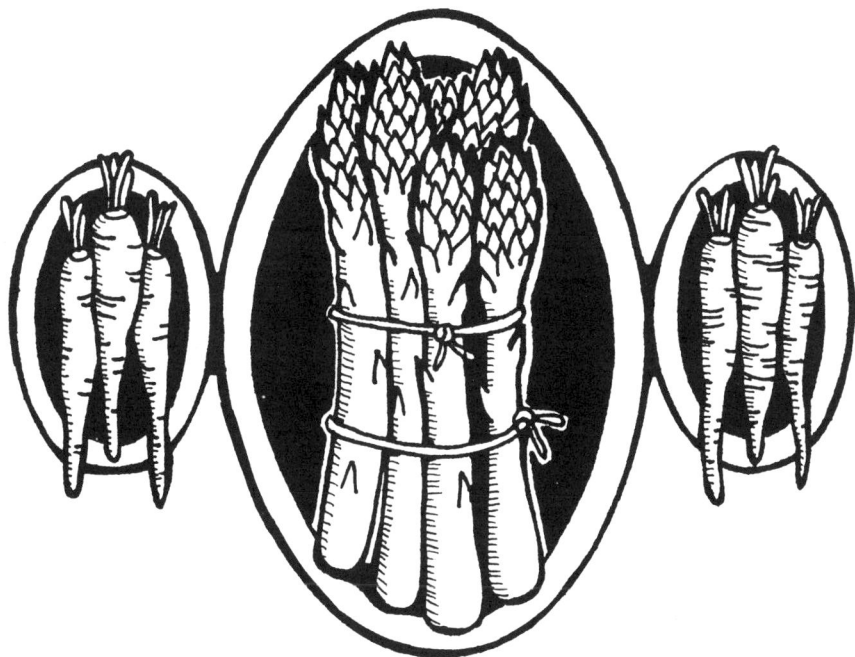

Useful Contacts In Israel

Animal Rights

Anonymous
P. O. Box 6315, Tel Aviv 61062   (03) 525-4632
48a Ben Yehuda Street, Tel Aviv
> Operates an educational center with information
> on animal rights and the environment.

Cat Lovers in Israel
P.O. Box 3858, Haifa 31037   (04) 244-724

Cat Welfare Society
Moshav Gan Haim 44910   (09) 917-329

Concern For Helping Animals in Israel (CHAI)
Tel Aviv   (03) 966-1121

Eilat Loves Animals
P.O. Box 3129, Eilat 88130   (07) 375-957

Heart For Animals
58 Dizengoff Street, Tel Aviv   (03) 298-255

Israel Horse Protection Society
P.O. Box 3038, Herzylia 46103

Israel Society for the Protection of Animals (shelters):

159 Herzl Street, Tel Aviv (Tel Aviv - Jaffa area)	(03) 682-7621
4 Hafez Haim Street, Tel Aviv (Ramat Gan area)	(03) 696-7394
P.O. Box 4009, Jerusalem (Atarot Industrial area)	(02) 851-531
P.O. Box 5334, Haifa	(04) 729-696
65 Rupin Street, Beer Sheva 63457	(07) 424-970

P.O. Box 2301, Rehovot 76122 (08) 464-564

P.O. Box 166, Raanana (HaSharon area) (09) 445-532

Israeli Society for the Abolition of Vivisection
P.O. Box 519, Givatayim 53104

Let The Animals Live (branches):

240 Ben Yehuda Street, Tel Aviv (03) 604-6488

18A Maimon Street, Haifa 32585 (04) 222-874

25 Meir Nakar Street, Jerusalem 93803 (02) 733-970

ProAnimal
P.O. Box 2039, Rehovot 76100 (08) 467-632
> English language publication on animals,
> animal rights, vegetarianism, and related
> topics in Israel.

Roof for Animals
15 Reines Street, Holon 58346 (03) 556-4263

S.O.S. Animals
Ashturay Hafarchi 9, Tel Aviv (03) 544-1045

Vegetarian/Vegan Societies

International Jewish Vegetarian Society
8 Balfour Street, Jerusalem 92102   (02) 611-114

Israel Vegetarian & Vegan Movement
2 Levontin Street, Tel Aviv 65111   (03) 560-7774/560-4582

Organization for Biological and Organic Agriculture in Israel
121 HaHashmonaim Street, Tel Aviv 67011   (03) 561-0538

Environmental Organizations

Council for a Beautiful Israel
76-78 Bograshov Street, Tel Aviv 65429   (03) 294-242

EcoNet
P.O. Box 581, Karkur 37105   (06) 377-072

Israel Union for Environmental Defense
317 Hayarkon Street, Tel Aviv 63504   (03) 546-8099/449-941

Society for Protection of Nature in Israel (branches):
4 Hashfela Street, Tel Aviv 66183   (03) 375-063

13 Heleni Hamalkah Street, Jerusalem   (02) 252-357

8 Menachem Street, Haifa   (04) 664-135

A Vegetarian Hebrew - English Dictionary

(Note: In the transliteration, an *i* is the sound of a *double e* in English.)

Food Related Terms

Breakfast -- Aruchat Boker
Carrot -- Gezer
Cucumber -- Melaffafon
Cutlet -- Ketziza
Dairy -- Halavi
Dinner -- Aruchat Erev
Eggplant -- Hatzilim
Eggs -- Baytzim
Flour -- Hita
Food -- Ochel
Free Range Eggs -- Baytzim Organim
Grains -- D'ganim
Kosher -- Kasher
Kosher Certificate -- Teudat Kashrut
Lettuce -- Chasa
Lunch -- Aruchat Tzohori'im
Macrobiotic -- Macrobioti
Meal -- Arucha
Menu -- Tafrit
Milk -- Halav
Natural -- Tivi
Natural Ingredients -- Rechivim Tivi'im
No Smoking Area -- Azor l'lo ishun
Nuts -- Egozim
Organic -- Organi
Organic Products -- Motzrim Organim
Organic Vegetables -- Yirakot Organiot

Pie (sweet and non-sweet) -- Pashtida
Pure -- Tahor
Reservation -- Hazmana
Restaurant -- Misadah
Rice -- Orez
Shnitzel -- Shnitzel
Smoking -- Ishun
Soy -- Soya
Soy Milk -- Chalav Soya
Tempeh -- Tempeh
Tomato -- Agvania
Vegan -- Tivoni
Vegetables -- Yirakot
Vegetarian -- Tzimchoni
Vegetarianism -- Tzimchonot
Waiter/Waitress -- Meltzar (it)
Whole Wheat Flour -- Chitah Meleah
Without Fish -- Bli Dagim
Without Meat -- Bli Basar

General Terms

Animals -- Ba'ali Haim
Animal Rights -- Zchuyot Ba'ali Haim
Cat -- Chatul
Dog -- Kelev
Ecology -- Ekologiah
Excuse Me -- Slicha
Health -- Brioot
Hello, Goodbye, Peace -- Shalom
How Much? -- Camah Oleh?
Moral -- Moosari
No - Lo
Thank You! -- Todah Robah!
World -- Olam
Yes -- Ken
You are Welcome! -- B'vakasha

Foods & Definitions of Foods Commonly Found in Israel

Blintzes: Very thin pancakes rolled and filled with a variety of fillings.

Couscous: Made from durum wheat and milled to different degrees of fineness. It is not a whole grain since all of its bran and germ are removed during processing. Couscous is a very small, off white grain that cooks in minutes.

Falafel: An appetizer or sandwich filling usually served with tahini in pita bread. Falafel is round and made from cooked chickpeas.

Hummus: Is made out of pureed chickpeas, tahini, and various spices. It is often served as a spread with pita bread.

Macrobiotic: A type of diet based on Eastern philosophy where certain foods are eliminated. A macrobiotic diet sometimes includes fish so is not always vegetarian.

Miso soup: Miso is a fermented soybean paste made out of soybeans, salt, and a starter. The beans undergo a fermentation process and then are allowed to age in wooden barrels for about three years. Miso soup is made from miso, chopped vegetables, and broth.

Organic: Food grown without the use of pesticides.

Tabouli: Also known as tabouleh, is a salad made from bulgur, vegetables, and fresh herbs.

Tamari: A fermented form of soy sauce.

Techina: Also known as tahini, is sesame seed butter made from ground hulled sesame seeds. It is beige in color and used to prepare salad dressings, dips and spreads, gravies, soups, etc.

Tempeh: Is produced by fermenting pre-soaked and cooked soybeans and sometimes a grain with a culture called rhizopus. Tempeh can be fried, steamed, boiled, or baked and is often mixed with grains and vegetables in casseroles.

Tempura: Vegetarian tempura consists of vegetables dipped in a batter and deep fried. This is a Japanese-style dish.

Tofu: Also known as bean curd, is made by soaking soybeans then grinding them and putting them through a filter. The remaining mixture is heated and a coagulant is added, resulting in soy curd and whey. The soy curd is pressed to make a soft or hard tofu, which is then used in soups, salads, dips, spreads, entrees, and desserts.

Vegan: A person who, in addition to being vegetarian, does not use other animal products and by-products including eggs, dairy products, and honey.

Vege burger: A non-meat patty usually made from one or more of the following ingredients: grains, nuts, soybeans, wheat gluten, and vegetables.

Vege fajita: A vegetarian version of this Latino dish consisting of thin pancakes filled with grilled vegetables and sometimes strips of tofu, tempeh, or wheat gluten.

Vege schnitzel: A vegetarian version of a dish traditionally made from veal, consisting of either tofu or wheat gluten.

Vegetarian: A person who does not eat meat, fish, or poultry.

The International Jewish Vegetarian Society

The International Jewish Vegetarian Society,
8 Balfour Street, Jerusalem 92102
Israel Telephone/Fax: (972) (02) 611-114.

✡ Why an International Jewish Vegetarian Society?

The International Jewish Vegetarian Society (IJVS) was founded to promote the vegetarian ideal and its relation to Jewish sources. (A vegetarian abstains from eating animal flesh including meat, fowl, and fish.) Their activities are focused on topical areas in Judaism that relate to vegetarianism. These include: health issues (proper nutrition, health implications of meat eating), the environment (decreased water and land usage, pollution), and compassion towards animals. They believe that as more people adopt a vegetarian lifestyle, we will increase the level of compassion towards all creatures on earth, including human beings.

✡ What are IJVS activities in Israel?

Their goal is to serve as a national address to support the estimated 120,000 vegetarians in Israel (2.5% of the total population). They also sponsor educational campaigns about the benefits of the vegetarian diet as well as the idea of Jewish vegetarianism. Their target audience includes the medical community (nutritionists, medical doctors, and dietitians), new immigrants (especially Russian olim), youth, the religious community, and the population at large. The IJVS offers lectures, food demonstrations, and other activities at its headquarters in Jerusalem.

Since the focus of the IJVS is both Israeli and international, they are also closely connected with both Jewish and non-Jewish vegetarian organizations in North America, Europe, and throughout the world. In Israel, they provide a forum for distributing the resources of these organizations, including books and videos, and for sponsoring overseas lecturers.

✡ Famous Jewish Vegetarians:

Did you know that the following were vegetarians and supporters of IJVS? Haifa Chief Rabbi Shear Yashuv Cohen, the late Shlomo Goren (former Ashkenazic Chief Rabbi of Israel), Rabbi David Rosen (ADL Community Relations Representative and former Chief Rabbi of Ireland), Mordechai Ben Porat (ex-Member of Knesset), Shmuel Jacobson (Secretary of the Knesset), and the late Isaac Bashevis Singer (author).

✡ As an IJVS member in Israel you are entitled to receive:

The **JEWISH VEGETARIAN Magazine** (in English) published in London.

Discounts at stores and restaurants affiliated with the International Jewish Vegetarian Society (IJVS) in Israel and abroad.

Discounts at all International Jewish Vegetarian Society (IJVS) events in Israel and abroad.

Local Mailings from their Jerusalem office.

Access to their **Library**.

Please call in advance to arrange a visit to the Center: (972) (02) 611-114

About the Author

Mark Weintraub is a freelance writer and consultant dedicated to the need to protect the earth's creatures and environment and to promote our health, well being, and compassion by adopting a vegetarian diet and lifestyle. Mark was the first Executive Director and a founder of the International Jewish Vegetarian Society's (IJVS) Jerusalem Center. Prior to his work at IJVS, he was Assistant Director of Orr Shalom, which runs vegetarian group homes for abused and neglected children in Jerusalem.

Mark immigrated to Israel from New York, having worked previously for the national United Jewish Appeal (UJA), where he participated in humanitarian ventures such as Operation Moses -- the secret airlift of Ethiopian Jews to Israel.

Mark has a Master's Degree in Public Administration and a Bachelor of Arts in Political Science. He is a licensed New York City tour guide specializing in tours of Jewish New York.

Mark currently resides with his wife Ina and their two cats, Mitch and Beebers, in Rosh Ha'ayin -- a small city of primarily Yemenite Jews north of Tel Aviv.

Resources in the United States

Concern for Animals in Israel
P.O. Box 3341, Alexandria, VA 22302   (703) 658-9650

Jewish Vegetarians of North America
6938 Reliance Road   (410) 754-5550
Federalsburg, MD 21632

> The purpose of Jewish Vegetarians of North America is to promote the practice of vegetarianism within the Judaic tradition, and explore the relationship between Judaism, dietary laws, and vegetarianism.

Jews for Animal Rights
255 Humphrey Street   (617) 631-7601
Marblehead, MA 01945

The Vegetarian Resource Group
P.O. Box 1463, Baltimore, MD 21203   (410) 366-8343
    (410) 366-8804 Fax

e-mail: TheVRG@aol.com

World Wide Web:
    http://envirolink.org/arrs/VRG/home.html

What is The Vegetarian Resource Group?

Our health professionals, activists, and educators work with businesses and individuals to bring about healthy changes in your school, workplace, and community. Registered dietitians and physicians aid in the development of practical, nutrition-related publications and answer member or media questions about the vegetarian diet.

Vegetarian Journal **is one of the benefits members enjoy.** Readers receive practical tips for vegetarian meal planning, articles on vegetarian nutrition, recipes, natural food product reviews, and an opportunity to share ideas with others. All nutrition articles are reviewed by a registered dietitian or medical doctor.

The Vegetarian Resource Group is a non-profit organization. Financial support comes primarily from memberships, contributions, and book sales. **Membership includes the bimonthly** *Vegetarian Journal*. **To join, send $20 to The Vegetarian Resource Group, P.O. Box 1463, Baltimore, MD 21203.**

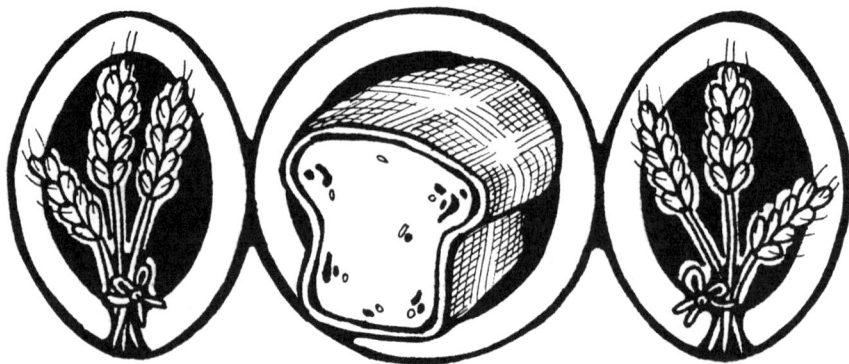

Other Books Available From The Vegetarian Resource Group

If you wish to purchase one or more of the following VRG titles, please send a check or money order made payable to *The Vegetarian Resource Group* (Maryland residents must add 5% sales tax) and mail it with your order to: *The Vegetarian Resource Group, P.O. Box 1463, Baltimore, MD 21203*. Make sure you include your mailing address. Or call (410) 366-8343 to order with MasterCard or VISA credit card. Price given includes postage in the United States. Outside the USA, please pay in US funds by credit card or money order and add $3.00 per book for postage and handling. Fax charge orders to (410) 366-8804.

SIMPLE, LOWFAT & VEGETARIAN

Unbelievably Easy Ways to Reduce the Fat in Your Meals!
by Suzanne Havala, M.S., R.D.
Recipes by Mary Clifford, R.D.
Foreword by Dean Ornish, M.D.

An easy-to-use guidebook to lowfat eating. How to enjoy Chinese, Mexican, Italian, Indian, and fast food. Chapters on bag lunches, amusement parks, pizza, movies, cafeterias, salad bars, planes, trains, cruise ships, and more. For each type of eating, *Menu Magic* gives you a few simple changes to reduce the fat in a typical meal. Additional help with *Good Choices, Fat Content of Selected Items*, and *Helpful Hints*. Includes shopping lists, recipes, 30 days of quick meals, over 100 lowfat brands found in natural foods stores, weight loss chapters, ideas for vegans, and help in revising your own recipes.

TRADE PAPERBACK, $14.95

SIMPLE, LOWFAT & VEGETARIAN

Unbelievably Easy Ways to Reduce the Fat in Your Meals!

❖ by Suzanne Havala, M.S., R.D. ❖

Recipes by
Mary Clifford, R.D.

Foreword by
Dean Ornish, M.D.

SIMPLE CHANGES
TO CUT BACK ON FAT WHEN:
- Eating Out
- Cooking at Home
- Shopping
- At Work or in School
- Going to the Movies
- Eating in Chinese Restaurants
- Enjoying Mexican Cuisine
- Dining Italian
- On Planes, Trains & Cruise Ships
- Plus much more...

MEATLESS MEALS FOR WORKING PEOPLE

Quick and Easy Vegetarian Recipes
by Debra Wasserman & Charles Stahler

Featured on Cable News Network (CNN)!
Vegetarian cooking can be simple or complicated. *The Vegetarian Resource Group* recommends using whole grains and fresh vegetables whenever possible. However, for the busy working person, this isn't always possible. Meatless Meals For Working People contains over 100 delicious, fast, and easy recipes, plus ideas which teach you how to be a vegetarian within your hectic schedule by using common, convenient, vegetarian foods. This handy guide also contains a spice chart, party ideas, information on fast food chains, and much more.

TRADE PAPERBACK, $6

NO CHOLESTEROL PASSOVER RECIPES

by Debra Wasserman

For many, low-calorie Passover recipes are a challenge. Here is a wonderful collection of Passover dishes that are non-dairy, eggless, no-cholesterol, and vegetarian. It includes recipes for eggless blintzes, dairyless carrot cream soup, festive macaroons, apple latkes, sweet and sour cabbage, knishes, broccoli with almond sauce, mock "chopped liver," no oil lemon dressing, eggless matzo meal pancakes, and much more. Includes nutritional analysis for the 100 vegan recipes.

PAPERBACK, $8.95

By Debra Wasserman

THE LOWFAT JEWISH VEGETARIAN COOKBOOK
HEALTHY TRADITIONS FROM AROUND THE WORLD

by Debra Wasserman

Featured on ABC's Good Morning America Show!
This 224-page book features over 150 lowfat Jewish vegetarian recipes with an international flavor, as well as menu ideas. The recipes do not contain dairy or eggs. A nutritional analysis is given for each recipe. Readers can sample such dishes as Romanian Apricot Dumplings, Lebanese Potato Salad, Czechoslovakian Noodles with Poppy Seeds, Moroccan Chickpea and Lentil Soup, Armenian Stuffed Eggplant, Polish Apple Blintzes, Potato Knishes, Indian Curry and Rice, Greek Pastry, and Spinach Pies. Celebrate with Eggless Challah, Hamentashen for Purim, Passover Vegetable Kishke, Chanukah Latkes, Russian Charoset, Mock Chopped "Liver," Eggless Matzoh Balls, and much more. Also includes Rosh Hashanah dinner suggestions, a glossary of foods used in Jewish vegetarian cooking, and lists of the top ten recipes for calcium and iron.

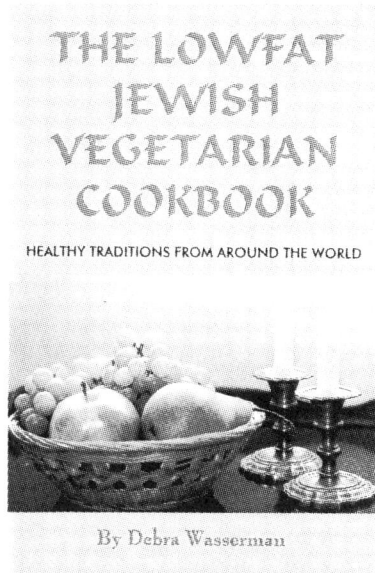

THE LOWFAT
JEWISH
VEGETARIAN
COOKBOOK

HEALTHY TRADITIONS FROM AROUND THE WORLD

By Debra Wasserman

TRADE PAPERBACK, $15

VEGETARIAN QUANTITY RECIPES
From The Vegetarian Resource Group

Here is a helpful kit for people who must cook for large groups and institutional settings. It contains 28 vegetarian recipes, including main dishes, burgers, sandwich spreads, side dishes, soups, salads, desserts, and breakfast foods. Each recipe provides servings for 25 and 50 people, and a nutritional analysis. The kit also contains a listing of companies offering vegetarian food items in institutional sizes and "Tips For Introducing Vegetarian Food Into Institutions."

PACKET, $15

SIMPLY VEGAN
QUICK VEGETARIAN MEALS

by Debra Wasserman
Nutrition Section by Reed Mangels, Ph.D., R.D.

Second Edition!
Over 35,000 copies sold of the first edition.
An easy-to-use vegetarian guide that contains over 160 kitchen-tested vegan recipes (no meat, fish, fowl, dairy, or eggs.) Each recipe is accompanied by a nutritional analysis. Reed Mangels, Ph.D., R.D., has included an extensive vegan nutrition section on topics such as Protein, Fat, Calcium, Iron, Vitamin B12, Pregnancy and the Vegan Diet, Feeding Vegan Children, and Calories, Weight Gain, and Weight Loss. A Nutritional Glossary is provided, along with sample menus, meal plans, and a list of the top recipes for iron, calcium, and Vitamin C. Also featured are food definitions and origins, and a comprehensive list of mail-order companies that specialize in selling vegan food, animal-free clothing, cruelty-free cosmetics, and ecologically-safe household products.

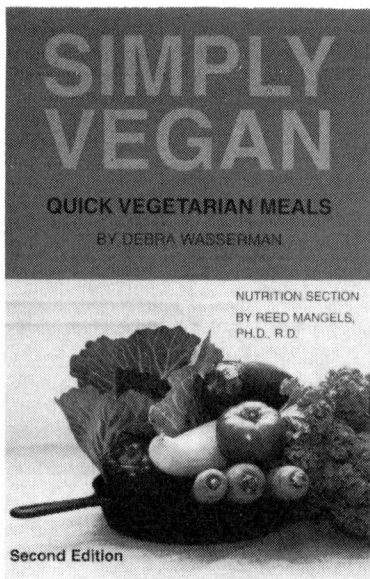

TRADE PAPERBACK. $12.95

THE VEGETARIAN GAME

This computer software educational game contains 750 questions. Learn while having fun. Categories include health/nutrition, how food choices affect the environment, animals and ethical choices, vegetarian foods, famous vegetarians, and potluck. Three age levels: 5 - 9; 10 or older/adults new to vegetarianism; and individuals with advanced knowledge of vegetarianism or anyone looking for a challenge. IBM PC-compatible, with CGA or better or Hercules graphics MS DOS 2.0 or higher.

SOFTWARE. $20.00

(When ordering, indicate 3.5" or 5.25" disk.)

THE VEGETARIAN GAME

Learn while having fun! Test your knowledge with 750 questions:
Health and Nutrition; Famous Vegetarians
How Food Choices Affect the Environment
Animals and Ethical Choices
Vegetarian Foods; Pot Luck

Three levels: Children ages 5 to 9; Ages 10 to Adult new to vegetarianism;
Anyone with advanced knowledge of vegetarianism or individuals looking for a challenge

IBM PC and 100% compatibles with CGA	ISBN 0-931411-11-4	VR!
or better or Hercules graphics	$19.95	
MS Dos 2.0 or higher	The Vegetarian Resource Group	
☐ 3.5" disk	PO Box 1463	
☐ 5.25" disk	Baltimore, MD 21203	

VEGETARIAN JOURNAL'S GUIDE TO NATURAL FOODS RESTAURANTS IN THE U.S. AND CANADA

OVER 2,000 LISTINGS OF RESTAURANTS & VACATION SPOTS

For the health-conscious traveler, this is the perfect traveling companion to ensure a great meal -- or the ideal lodgings -- when away from home. And for those who are looking for a nearby place to eat, this unique guide offers a host of new and interesting possibilities. As people have become more health-conscious, there has been a delightful proliferation of restaurants designed to meet the growing demand for healthier meals. To help locate these places, there is now a single source for information on over 2,000 restaurants, vacation resorts, and more.

The Vegetarian Journal's Guide to Natural Foods Restaurants (Avery Publishing Group, Inc.) is a helpful guide listing eateries state by state and province by province. Each entry not only describes the house specialties, varieties of cuisine, and special dietary menus, but also includes information on ambiance, attire, and reservations. It even tells you whether or not you can pay by credit card. And there's more. Included in this guide are listings of vegetarian inns, spas, camps, tours, travel agencies, and vacation spots.

PAPERBACK, $13

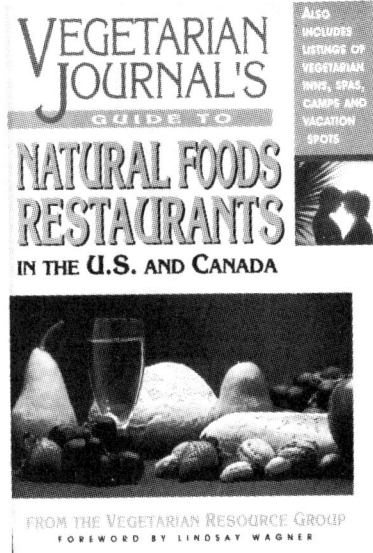

VEGETARIAN JOURNAL'S FOOD SERVICE UPDATE NEWSLETTER

This three-times-a-year newsletter is for food service personnel and others working for healthier food in schools, restaurants, hospitals, and other institutions. Vegetarian Journal's Food Service Update Newsletter offers advice, shares recipes, and spotlights leaders in the industry who are providing the healthy options consumers are seeking.

One Year Subscription, $20; $5 with Vegetarian Journal Subscription

Leprechaun Cake and Other Tales
A Vegetarian Story - Cookbook

Stories and Pictures by Vonnie Winslow Crist
Recipes by Debra Wasserman

This story-cookbook is suitable for children ages eight through eleven, but grown-ups love the stories and recipes, too. Included are four multi-cultural fantasy tales, as well as over 40 vegan recipes. Learn to accept others from different backgrounds by sharing stories and good-tasting food. Enjoy Bina and David's favorite recipes: Rainy Day Lemonade, Leprechaun Cake, Fruit French Toast, North African Pea Dish, and Mrs. Prabhu's Rice Pudding. Help Mitsue cheer up her grandmother at a Fourth of July Parade and Picnic (with a little assistance from Lucky the Dragon).

Leprechaun Cake and Other Tales
A Vegetarian Story-Cookbook

Stories and Pictures by
Vonnie Winslow Crist
Recipes By **Debra Wasserman**

Brighten your day by making Quick Fireworks Salsa, Dragon Party Punch, and Tia's Favorite Applesauce. Visit South America with Deer and Jaguarundi for a lesson about friendship. Join their feast with Mexican Succotash, Jaguar's Wedding Stew, and Frozen Banana Treat. Meet a lonely Snow Queen and caring troll. Discover that unicorns, like people of all nationalities must run free. Celebrate the freedom to be who you are by sharing Troll's Tasty Hot Apple Cider, Syrian Wheat Pudding, and Unicorn's Golden Chutney.

Trade Paperback, $9.95

VEGETARIAN JOURNAL REPORTS
Edited by Debra Wasserman & Charles Stahler

This 112-page book consists of the best articles from previous *Vegetarian Journals*. Included are a 28-Day Meal Plan, a Vegetarian Weight Loss Guide, Tips for Changing Your Diet, a Vegetarian Guide for Athletes, Information for Diabetic Diets, plus Indian Recipes, Eggless Dishes, and many more vegetarian resources.

PAPERBACK, $12

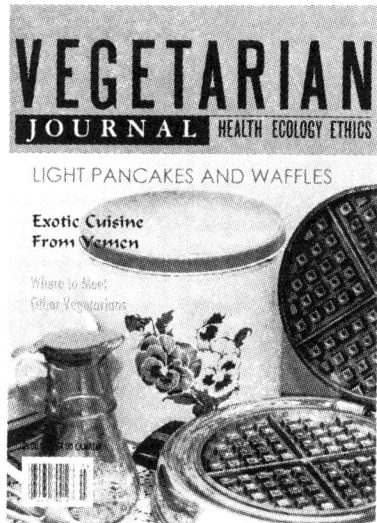

The following books are published by Micah Publications and available from The Vegetarian Resource Group.

JUDAISM AND VEGETARIANISM
By Richard H. Schwartz

This 204-page book covers a wide variety of topics including Judaism and Compassion for Animals; Preserving Health and Life; Feeding the Hungry; and Judaism, Vegetarianism, and Ecology. Biographies of Famous Jewish Vegetarians are included, as well as a recipe section.

Paperback, $14

HAGGADAH FOR THE LIBERATED LAMB
Edited by Roberta Kalechofsky

This 160-page Hebrew/English Haggadah can be used at a Passover Seder. It incorporates animal welfare messages throughout the book.

Paperback, $15

HAGGADAH FOR THE VEGETARIAN FAMILY
Edited by Roberta Kalechofsky

Here's another Hebrew/English Haggadah that can be used at a Passover Seder. This book is shorter than the book above and easier for children to follow.

Paperback, $10

RABBIS AND VEGETARIANISM: AN EVOLVING TRADITION
Edited by Roberta Kalechofsky

This anthology of 17 essays by Orthodox, Conservative, Reform, and Reconstructionist Rabbis contains the theme that vegetarianism is the new kashrut. The book is 104 pages.

Paperback, $10

OTHER ISRAELI TRAVEL GUIDES THAT WILL MAKE YOUR TRIP A SUCCESS!

Bazak Guide to Israel, 1994-95. Produced by Avraham and Ruth Levi. HarperCollins, Publishers, 1993.

Essential Jerusalem. By Greer Fay Gashman. Passport Books, 1994.

*A **Guide to Hiking in Israel***. By Joel Roskin. The Jerusalem Post, 1994.

Insight Guides: Jerusalem. By Norman Atkins. Houghton Mifflin Company, 1995.

Israeli Guide. By Stephanie Gold. Open Road Publishing, 1996.

Let's Go: The Budget Guide to Israel and Egypt, 1996. Edited by Jed Willard. St. Martin's Press, 1996.

Israeli Vegetarian Restaurant Guide Survey

1. Restaurant Name: _____

2. Address: _____
   (Enclose map or directions if not located in central location)

3. Telephone Number: _____

4. Type of Restaurant (check all that are relevant):

❏ Vegetarian (no meat, fish, or fowl)   ❏ Vegan (no meat, fish, fowl, dairy, eggs, or other animal products)
❏ Macrobiotic   ❏ Dairy Only   ❏ Dairy and Fish   ❏ Natural Foods   ❏ Other
❏ Ethnic Specialty (ex. Italian, Oriental, Indian, other) _____

5. Organic products and/or natural unprocessed ingredients are used in:
   ❏ Some   ❏ Many   ❏ All of your dishes.

6. Do you serve any dishes that are totally vegan (no dairy, eggs)?
   ❏ Yes   ❏ No   If yes, please describe dish (or circle on menu):
   _____

7. Description/Special Features (unique foods, fresh baked bread, decor, music, view, location, history) What makes your restaurant special?
   _____
   _____

8. Hours: _____

9. Meals served: _____

10. Type of Service (check all that are relevant):
    ❏ Full Service (regular table service)   ❏ Self-serve   ❏ Take-out   ❏ Catering

11. What type of kosher certification do you have? _____

12.   ❏ Non-Smoking   ❏ Smoking Allowed   ❏ Smoking Area

13. Reservations: ❏   Required   ❏ Not needed   Do you accommodate large groups? _____

14. Method of Payment: ❏ Credit Card   ❏ Traveler's Checks   ❏ Foreign Currency   ❏ NIS only
    Credit Cards Accepted: _____

15. Meal Cost per Person (based on price of average entree): _____

16. Person filling out survey: _____

Include a Menu and any descriptive material with the survey form.

Please return survey form to:
The Vegetarian Resource Group, P.O. Box 1463, Baltimore, MD 21203, USA
or Fax to: (410) 366-8804

Israeli Vegetarian Restaurant Guide Survey

1. Restaurant Name: _____

2. Address: _____
   (Enclose map or directions if not located in central location)

3. Telephone Number: _____

4. Type of Restaurant (check all that are relevant):

❑ Vegetarian (no meat, fish, or fowl)   ❑ Vegan (no meat, fish, fowl, dairy, eggs, or other animal products)
❑ Macrobiotic   ❑ Dairy Only   ❑ Dairy and Fish   ❑ Natural Foods   ❑ Other
❑ Ethnic Specialty (ex. Italian, Oriental, Indian, other) _____

5. Organic products and/or natural unprocessed ingredients are used in:
   ❑ Some   ❑ Many   ❑ All of your dishes.

6. Do you serve any dishes that are totally vegan (no dairy, eggs)?
   ❑ Yes   ❑ No   If yes, please describe dish (or circle on menu):

_____

7. Description/Special Features (unique foods, fresh baked bread, decor, music, view, location, history) What makes your restaurant special?

_____
_____

8. Hours: _____

9. Meals served: _____

10. Type of Service (check all that are relevant):
    ❑ Full Service (regular table service)   ❑ Self-serve   ❑ Take-out   ❑ Catering

11. What type of kosher certification do you have? _____

12.   ❑ Non-Smoking   ❑ Smoking Allowed   ❑ Smoking Area

13. Reservations: ❑ Required   ❑ Not needed   Do you accommodate large groups? _____

14. Method of Payment: ❑ Credit Card   ❑ Traveler's Checks   ❑ Foreign Currency   ❑ NIS only
    Credit Cards Accepted: _____

15. Meal Cost per Person (based on price of average entree): _____

16. Person filling out survey: _____

Include a Menu and any descriptive material with the survey form.

Please return survey form to:
The Vegetarian Resource Group, P.O. Box 1463, Baltimore, MD 21203, USA
or Fax to: (410) 366-8804

Travel Notes

Travel Notes

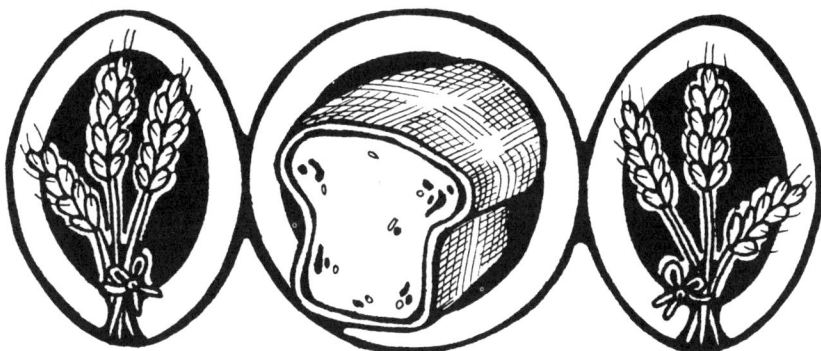

Additional Copies of

Guide to Vegetarian Restaurants in Israel

may be purchased by sending $9.95
postage included
(Maryland Residents add 5% sales tax) to:

The Vegetarian Resource Group
P.O. Box 1463, Baltimore, MD 21203
Inquire about orders in quantity

*For postage & handling outside
the United States, add $3.00*

VR^g.

To join

The Vegetarian Resource Group
and Receive the Bimonthly
Vegetarian Journal
for One Year

Send $20.00 to the Above Address
(Canadian/Mexican subscriptions - Send $30.00
Other Foreign Country subscriptions - Send $42.00)